W9-BBJ-762

PENGUIN POETS

# BOOK OF BLUES

Jack Kerouac was born in Lowell, Massachusetts, in 1922, the youngest of three children in a Franco-American family. He attended local Catholic and public schools and won a football scholarship to Columbia University in New York City, where he first met Neal Cassady, Allen Ginsberg, and William S. Burroughs. He quit school in his sophomore year after a dispute with his football coach, and joined the Merchant Marine, beginning the restless wanderings that were to continue for the greater part of his life. His first novel, *The Town and the City*, appeared in 1950, but it was *On the Road*, first published in 1957 and memorializing his adventures with Neal Cassady, that epitomized to the world what became known as "the Beat generation" and made Kerouac one of the most controversial and best-known writers of his time. Publication of his many other books followed, among them *The Dharma Bums*, *The Subterraneans*, and *Big Sur*. Kerouac considered them all to be part of *The Duluoz Legend*. "In my old age," he wrote, "I intend to collect all my work and reinsert my pantheon of uniform names, leave the long shelf full of books there, and die happy." He died in St. Petersburg, Florida, in 1969, at the age of forty-seven.

*By Jack Kerouac*

The Town and the City
The Scripture of the Golden Eternity
Some of the Dharma
Old Angel Midnight
Good Blonde and Others
Pull My Daisy
Trip Trap
Pic
The Portable Jack Kerouac
Selected Letters: 1940–1956
Selected Letters: 1957–1969
Atop an Underwood
Orpheus Emerged

POETRY

Mexico City Blues
Scattered Poems
Pomes All Sizes
Heaven and Other Poems
Book of Blues
Book of Haikus

THE DULUOZ LEGEND

Visions of Gerard
Doctor Sax
Maggie Cassidy
Vanity of Duluoz
On the Road
Visions of Cody
The Subterraneans
Tristessa
Lonesome Traveller
Desolation Angels
The Dharma Bums
Book of Dreams
Big Sur
Satori in Paris

*JACK KEROUAC*

# BOOK OF BLUES

PENGUIN POETS

PENGUIN BOOKS
Published by the Penguin Group
Penguin Group (USA) Inc., 375 Hudson Street, New York, New York 10014, U.S.A.
Penguin Group (Canada), 90 Eglinton Avenue East, Suite 700, Toronto,
Ontario, Canada M4P 2Y3 (a division of Pearson Penguin Canada Inc.)
Penguin Books Ltd, 80 Strand, London WC2R 0RL, England
Penguin Ireland, 25 St Stephen's Green, Dublin 2, Ireland (a division of Penguin Books Ltd)
Penguin Group (Australia), 250 Camberwell Road, Camberwell,
Victoria 3124, Australia (a division of Pearson Australia Group Pty Ltd)
Penguin Books India Pvt Ltd, 11 Community Centre, Panchsheel Park, New Delhi – 110 017, India
Penguin Group (NZ), cnr Airborne and Rosedale Roads,
Albany, Auckland 1310, New Zealand (a division of Pearson New Zealand Ltd)
Penguin Books (South Africa) (Pty) Ltd, 24 Sturdee Avenue,
Rosebank, Johannesburg 2196, South Africa

Penguin Books Ltd, Registered Offices: 80 Strand, London WC2R 0RL, England

First published in Penguin Books 1995

20

Copyright © Estate of Stella Kerouac, John Sampas, Literary Representative, 1995
Introduction copyright © Robert Creeley, 1995
All rights reserved

Grateful acknowledgment is made for permission to reprint the following copyrighted works:
Selection from *Jack Kerouac* by Tom Clark. Copyright © 1984 by Tom Clark.
By permission of Marlowe & Company.
Selection from "Statement on Poetics for *The New American Poetry*"
from *Good Blonde & Others* by Jack Kerouac. © 1993, by permission of Grey Fox Press.
Selection from *Understanding the Beats* by Edward Halsey Foster.
By permission of the University of South Carolina Press.
"Jack Would Speak Through the Imperfect Medium of Alice" from *Selected Poems of Alice Notley*, Talisman House, Publishers, 1993. Reprinted by permission of the publisher. Copyright © 1993 by Alice Notley.

LIBRARY OF CONGRESS CATALOGING IN PUBLICATION DATA
Kerouac, Jack, 1922–1969.
Book of blues / Jack Kerouac.
p. cm.—(Penguin poets)
Contents: San Francisco blues—Richmond Hill blues—Bowery blues—Macdougal Street blues—Desolation blues—Orizaba 210 blues—Orlanda blues—Cerrada Medellin blues.
ISBN 0 14 05.8700 4
1. Beat generation—Poetry. I. Title.
PS3521.E735B55 1995
811'.54—dc20 94–45902

Printed in the United States of America
Set in Sabon
Designed by Ann Gold

Except in the United States of America, this book is sold subject to the condition that it shall not, by way of trade or otherwise, be lent, resold, hired out, or otherwise circulated without the publisher's prior consent in any form of binding or cover other than that in which it is published and without a similar condition including this condition being imposed on the subsequent purchaser.

The scanning, uploading and distribution of this book via the Internet or via any other means without the permission of the publisher is illegal and punishable by law. Please purchase only authorized electronic editions, and do not participate in or encourage electronic piracy of copyrighted materials. Your support of the author's rights is appreciated.

*This book is dedicated to Philip Whalen*
*and to the memory of Lew Welch*

# CONTENTS

*Introduction by Robert Creeley* ix

SAN FRANCISCO BLUES 3

RICHMOND HILL BLUES 82

BOWERY BLUES 97

MACDOUGAL STREET BLUES 107

DESOLATION BLUES 117

ORIZABA 210 BLUES 129

ORLANDA BLUES 201

CERRADA MEDELLIN BLUES 249

*Notes on Dates and Sources* 271

*"Jack Would Speak Through the Imperfect Medium of Alice," by Alice Notley* 273

# CONTENTS

# INTRODUCTION

Hard now to go back to the time when Jack Kerouac was writing these poems, the fifties and early sixties, and to the way people then felt poetry *should* be written and what they thought it *should* be saying. Perhaps it hardly matters that much of the poetry of that time found little popular audience, or that it spoke in a way that often confounded its readers. There was a high culture and a low one, and poetry was something significantly attached to the former. The rest was just the passing blur of pop songs and singers, or else the shady edges of black culture and its curiously enduring jazz. Great composers like Stravinsky might use such "forms" for context, and might even get someone like Benny Goodman to play the results. But it always seemed an isolated instance—if not overt slumming.

That was the problem, in fact, not only with music, or poetry, but with writing itself. There was an intense orthodoxy, an insistent critical watchguard, patrolling the borders of legitimate literature to keep all in their necessary places. If one came from habits or ways of speaking or thinking that weren't of the requisite pattern, then the response was abrupt and hostile. Even a poet as Kenneth Rexroth, admitting his complex relation to Kerouac from their times together in San Francisco, wrote of *Mexico City Blues* (1959) that it constituted a "naive effrontery" to have published it as poetry, and that it was "more pitiful than ridiculous." Donald M. Allen's break-through anthology, *The New American Poetry* (1960), soon made clear the resources and authority of what Kerouac and others of his situation were doing, but for a time it seemed that even the viable elders would prove too fixed in their aspirations or disappointments to recognize its authority.

What was the common dream? To be enough of whatever was wanted, to be real, to be included. That meant thinking and talking and moving in one's own legitimacy, one's own given "world," with its persons, habits, humor and place. It was Ginsberg who early on valued particularly Kerouac's crucial insight, that one might write in the same words and manner that one would use in talking to a friend. There didn't have to be a rhetorical "heightening," or a remove from the common, the intimate, and the personal.

Kerouac's friends were then specifically the poets: Allen Ginsberg, Gregory Corso, Philip Lamantia, Gary Snyder, Philip Whalen, Lawrence Ferlinghetti, Michael McClure, Bob Kaufman, Diane di Prima, Lew Welch, Amiri Baraka—and so on through a list now familiar indeed. In contrast, only the novelists John Clellon Holmes and William Burroughs (a source and company for all that "Beat" defined) were in any sense so alert and securing in their relations to him. His sister Caroline ("Nin") and his mother were otherwise safe havens, and he left and returned to their company again and again. Two of the sequences here, "Richmond Hill Blues" (1953) and "Orlanda Blues" (1958), were written while living in his mother's house. The fact of all these relations sounds persistently throughout his writing, and in the poems it is especially emphatic. "Eleven Verses of Garver," (in the section "Orizaba 210 Blues") is literally that, the stories of his friend Bill Garver, described by Kerouac's perceptive biographer Tom Clark (*Jack Kerouac*, 1984) as "a garrulous, aging junkie who occupied the ground-floor apartment" at Orizaba 210, Mexico City, while Kerouac lived in the "mud block" (his words) on the roof. Clark notes it is in this circumstance that Kerouac works as well on *Mexico City Blues* and begins the novel of his "chaste, desperate courtship" of Bill Garver's connection for morphine, *Tristessa* (1960).

All such detail has been usefully spelled out in the various accounts of Kerouac's life. His own sense of what he was doing, either with prose or poems, is equally to the point. In his "Statement on Poetics" for *The New American Poetry* he writes: "Add alluvials to the end of your line when all is exhausted but something has to be said for some specified irrational reason, since reason can never win out, because poetry is NOT a science. The rhythm of how you 'rush' yr statement determines the rhythm of the poem, whether it is a poem in verse-separated lines, or an endless one-line poem called prose . . ." Of course, the parallel is clearly jazz. Thus Edward Foster in his useful work, *Understanding the Beats* (1992), emphasizes Kerouac's own proposal of the relation as follows:

> In a note at the beginning of [*Mexico City Blues*], Kerouac says that he wants "to be considered as a jazz poet blowing a long blues in an afternoon jazz session on Sunday," and the individual poems depend, like jazz pieces, on spontaneity and inspiration. Each of the 242 "choruses" is limited by the size of the notebook pages on which he wrote; if an idea (or riff) was not exhausted in that space, he would pick it up in the next poem . . .
>
> Most of the choruses are playful and light, and seemingly anything that fits the general drift of the rhythm, music, and tone can be added, no matter how incongruous it may seem: the sound of a bus outside the building ("Z a r o o o m o o o") an idea for Buddhist lipstick ("Nirvana–No"), nonsense language ("I'm a Agloon") . . . In any case, the poem expresses the poet's sensibility at the moment of writing, and the final poem [of *Mexico City Blues*] identifies "the sound in your mind" as an origin for song . . .

A complaint commonly lodged against Kerouac is that he was at best a self-taught "natural," at worst an example of the *cul de sac* the autodidact in the arts invariably comes to, a solipsistic "world" of his own limitations and confusions.

Blake, naked in his garden, was thus vulnerable. Céline, with his obsessive determination to outplot plot, was also a fool of such kind, as are all heroes of transformation and risk—Henry Miller, D. H. Lawrence and W.C. Williams among them. Otherwise it would be simply "minds like beds, always made up," as Williams said, an enclosure of all that might have been made articulate, felt, tasted, witnessed, and confessed as actual to one's own life, for better or for worse, at last.

But Kerouac was never simply an isolated writer in a time of classic authority and stylistic composure. If one considers Saul Bellow's *The Adventures of Augie March* (1953) in relation to *On the Road* (1957), one will understand precisely what William Burroughs means in saying of Kerouac:

> Kerouac was a writer. That is, he wrote. Many people who call themselves writers and have their names on books are not writers and they can't write—the difference being a bullfighter who fights a bull is different from the bullshitter who makes passes with no bull there. The writer has been *there* or he can't write about it. . . . Sometimes, as in the case of Fitzgerald and Kerouac, the effect produced by a writer is immediate, as if a generation were waiting to be written.

These poems provide an intensely vivid witness of both writer and time. Much is painful, even at times contemptible—the often violent disposition toward women, the sodden celebrations of drink—but it is nonetheless fact of a world still very much our own. Kerouac speaks its painful content, which is not to exempt him from a responsibility therefore. But a world is never simply a choice but a given, and it was not his intent to be brutal if that seems the point. Provincial, yet capable of effecting a common bond, of feeling a joy he could instantly make real for others, he lived in his world as particularly as anyone ever could. What holds it finally all together are *words*, one after another, as he plays, moves, with their sound, follows their lead, shifting from English to Franco-American *joual*, nonsense to sense, reflection to immediate sight and intimate record. He spoke no English until he was five. He wrote incessantly, carrying usually a small spiral notebook in his back pocket so as to "sketch" what occurred on the spot. He was in that old way "serious." He really believed in words.

So one will read here his various recording, invention, improvisation, story. Yet all will be mistaken, misunderstood, if there is not the recognition that this remarkable person is living here, is actual in all that is written. Another poet, Alice Notley, wrote some years after Jack Kerouac's death in 1969 a poem of singular power, "Jack Would Speak through the Imperfect Medium of Alice." This is its close:

> . . . The words are all only one word the perfect
> word—
> My body my alcohol my pain my death are only
> the perfect word as I
> Tell it to you, poor sweet categorizers
> Listen
> Every me I was & wrote
> were only & all (gently)
> That one perfect word

—Robert Creeley
Buffalo, N.Y.

moves, with their sound, follows their lead, shifting from English to Franco-American jonal, nonsense to sense, reflection to immediate sight and intimate record. He spoke no English until he was five. He wrote incessantly, carrying usually a small spiral notebook in his back pocket so as to "sketch" what occurred on the spot. He was in that old way "serious." He really believed in words.

So one will read here his various recording, invention, improvisation, story. Yet all will be misaken, misunderstood, if there is not the recognition that this remarkable person is living here, is actual in all that is written. Another poet, Alice Notley, wrote some years after Jack Kerouac's death in 1969 a poem of singular power, "Jack Would Speak through the Imperfect Medium of Alice." This is its closer:

> . . . The words are all only one word the perfect
> word—
> My body my alcohol my pain my death are only
> the perfect word as I
> Tell it to you, poor sweet categorizers
> Listen
> Every me I was & wrote
> were only & all (gently)
> That one perfect word

—Robert Creeley
Buffalo, N.Y.

In my system, the form of blues choruses is limited by the small page of the breastpocket notebook in which they are written, like the form of a set number of bars in a jazz blues chorus, and so sometimes the word-meaning can carry from one chorus into another, or not, just like the phrase-meaning can carry harmonically from one chorus to the other, or not, in jazz, so that, in these blues as in jazz, the form is determined by time, and by the musician's spontaneous phrasing & harmonizing with the beat of the time as it waves & waves on by in measured choruses.

It's all gotta be non stop ad libbing within each chorus, or the gig is shot.

—Jack Kerouac

# SAN FRANCISCO BLUES

## 1ST CHORUS

I see the backs
Of old Men rolling
Slowly into black
Stores.

## 2ND CHORUS

Line faced mustached
Black men with turned back
Army weathered brownhats
Stomp on by with bags
Of burlap & rue
Talking to secret
Companions with long hair
In the sidewalk
On 3rd Street
San Francisco
With the rain of exhaust
  Plicking in the mist
  You see in black
  Store doors—
  Petting trucks farting—
  Vastly city.

## 3RD CHORUS

3rd St Market to Lease
Has a washed down tile
Tile entrance once white
  Now caked with gum
Of a thousand hundred feet
Feet of passers who
  Did not go straight on
Bending to flap the time
Pap page on back
With smoke emanating
From their noses
But slowly like old
  Lantern jawed junkmen
  Hurrying with the lump
  Wondrous potato bag
    To the avenues of sunshine
    Came, bending to spit,
  & Shuffled awhile there.

## 4TH CHORUS

The rooftop of the beatup
tenement
On 3rd & Harrison
Has Belfast painted
Black on yellow
On the side
the old Frisco wood is
shown with weatherbeaten
rainboards & a
washed out blue bottle
once painted for wild
commercial reasons by
an excited seltzerite
as firemen came last
afternoon & raised the
ladder to a fruitless
fire that was not there,
so, is Belfast singin
in this time

## 5TH CHORUS

when brand's forgotten
  taste washed in
  rain the gullies broadened
  & every body gone
the acrobats of the
  tenement
   who dug bel fast
   divers all
  and the divers all dove

  ah
   little girls make
   shadows on the
   sidewalk shorter
  than the shadow
    of death
      in this town—

## 6TH CHORUS

Fat girls
In red coats
With flap white out shoes

  Monstrous soldiers
  Stalk at dawn
Looking for whores
  And burning to eat up

Harried Mexican Laborers
  Become respectable
  In San Francisco
Carrying newspapers
Of culture burden
And packages of need
Walk sadly reluctant
  To work in dawn
Stalking with not cat
In the feel of their stride
 Touching to hide the sidewalk,
 Blackshiny lastnight parlor
 Shoes hitting the slippery
With hard slicky heels
  To slide & Fall:
    Breboac! Karrak!

## 7TH CHORUS

Dumb kids with thick lips
And black skin
Carry paper bags
Meaninglessly:
"Stop bothering the cat!"
His mother yelled at him
Yesterday and now
He goes to work
Down Third Street
In the milky dawn
Piano rolling over the hill
To the tune of the English
Fifers in some whiter mine,
'Brick a brack,
Pliers on your back;
Mick mack
Kidneys in your back;
Bald Boo!
Oranges and you!
Lick lock
The redfaced cock'

## 8TH CHORUS

Oi yal!
She yawns to lall
La la—
Me Loom—
The weary gray hat
Peacoat ex sailor
Marining meekly
Hands a poop a pocket
Face
Lips
Oh Mo Sea!
The long fat yellow
Eternity cream
Of the Third St Bus
Roof swimming like
A monosyllable
Armored Mososaur
Swimming in my Primordial
Windowpane
Of pain

## 9TH CHORUS

Alas! Youth is worried,
Pa's astray.
What so say
  To well dressed ambassadors
  From death's truth
  Pimplike, rich,
  In the morning slick;
  Or sad white caps
  Of snowy sea men
  In San Francisco
Gray streets
  Arm waving to walk
  The Harrison cross
    And earn later sunset
    purple

## 10TH CHORUS

Dig the sad old bum
No money
Presuming to hit the store
And buy his cube of oleo
For 8 cents
So in cheap rooms
At A M 3 30
He can cough & groan
In a white tile sink
By his bed
Which is used
To run water in
And stagger to
In the reel of wake up
Middle of the night
Flophouse Nightmares—
His death no blackern
Mine, his Toast's
Just as well buttered
And on the one side.

## 11TH CHORUS

There's no telling
What's on the mind
Of the bony
Character in plaid
Workcoat & glasses
Carrying lunch
Stalking & bouncing
Slowly to his job

Or the beauteous Indian
Girl hurrying stately
Into Marathon Grocery
Run by Greeks
To buy bananas
For her love night,
What's she thinking?
Her lips are like cherries,
Her cheeks just purse them out
All the more to kiss them
And suck their juices out.

## 12TH CHORUS

A young woman flees an old man,
Mohammedan Prophecy:
And she got avocados
Anyhow.

The furtive whore
Looks over her shoulder
While unlocking the door
Of the tenement
Of her pimp
Who with big Negro Arkansas
Or East Texas Oilfields
Harry Truman hat's
Been standin on the street
All day
Waiting for the cold girl
Bending in thincoat in the wind
And Sunday afternoon drizzle
To step on it & get some bread
For Papa's gotta sleep tonite
And the Chinaman's coming back

## 13TH CHORUS

"No hunger & no wittles
neither deary"
Said the crone
To Edwin Drood

Okay.
There'll be an answer.
Forthcoming
When the morning wind
Ceases shaking
The man's collar
When there's no starch in't
And Acme Beer
Runs flowing
Into dry gray hats.
When
Dearie
The pennies in the
palm multiply
as you watch

## 14TH CHORUS

When whistlers stop scowling
Smokers stop sighing
Watchers stop looking
And women stop walking

When gray beards
Grow no more
And pain dont
Take you by surprise
And bedposts creak
In rhythm not at morn
And dry men's bones
Are not pushed
By angry meaning pelvic
Propelled legs of reason
To a place you hate,
Then I'll go lay my crown
Body on the heads of 3 men
Hurrying & laughing
In the wrong direction,
my Idol

## 15TH CHORUS

Sex is an automaton
Sounding like a machine
Thru the stopped up keyhole
—Young men go fastern
  Old men
  Old men are passionately
    breathless
 Young men breathe inwardly
 Young women & old women
 Wait

There was a sound of slapping
When the angel stole come
And the angel that had lost
  Lay back satisfied

Hungry addled red face
With tight clutch
  Traditional Time
  Brief case in his paw
Prowls placking the pavement
 To his office girl's
  Rumped skirt at 5's
    Five O Clock Shadows

## 16TH CHORUS

Angrily I must insist—
The phoney Negro
Sea captain
With the battered coat
Who looks like
Charley Chaplin in a
movie about now filmed
in the air by crews
of raving rabid
angels drooling happi
ly
among the funny fat
Cherubim
Leading that serious
Hardjawed sincere
Negro stud
In at morn
For a round of crimes
Is Lucifer the Fraud

## 17TH CHORUS

Little girls worry too much
For no one will hurt them
Except the beast
Whom they'd knife
In another life
In the as well East
As West of Bethlehem
And do of it much

Rhetorical Third Street
Grasping at racket
Groans & stinky
I've no time
To dally hassel
In your heart's house,
It's too gray
I'm too cold—
I wanta go to Golden,
That's my home.

## 18TH CHORUS

I came a wearyin
From eastern hills;
Yonder Nabathacaque recessit
The eastward to Aurora rolls,
Somewhere West of Idalia
Or east of Klamath Falls,
One—Lost a blackhaired
Woman with thin feet
And red bag hangin
Who usta walk
Down Arapahoe Street
In Denver
And made all the
cabbies cry
And drugstore ponies
Eating pool in Remsac's
Sob, to See so Lovely
All the Time
And all so Tight
And young.

## 19TH CHORUS

Pshaw! Paw's Ford
Got Lost in the Depression
He driv over the Divide
  And forgot to cleave the road
Instead put atomic energy
 In the ass of his machine
And flew to find
  The gory clouds
Of rocky torment
    Far away
    And they fished him
    Outa Miner's Creek
    More dead n Henry
    And a whole lot fonder,
    Podner—
      Clack of the wheel's
      My freight train blues

Third Street I seed

## 20TH CHORUS

And knowed
And under ramps I writ
The poems of the punk
Who met the Fagin
Who told him 'Punk
When walkin with me
To roll a Sleepin drunk
Dont wish ya was back
Home in yr mother's parlor
And when the cops
Come ablastin
With loaded 45's
Dont ask for gold
Or silver from my purse,
Its milken hassel
Will be strewn
And scattered
In the sand
By an old bean can
And dried up kegs
We'd a sat & jawed on—

## 21ST CHORUS

Roll my bones
In the Mortiary
My terms
And deeds of mortgagry
And death & taxes
All wrapt up.'

Little anger Japan
Strides holding bombs
To blow the West
To Fuyukama's
Shrouded Mountain Top
So the Lotus Bubble
Blossoms in Buddha's
Temple Dharma Eye
May unfold from
Pacific Center
Inward Out & Over
The Essence Center World

## 22ND CHORUS

For the world's an Eye
And the universe is Seeing
Liquid
Rare
Radiant.

Eccentrics from out of town
Better not fill in
This blank
For a job on my gray boat
And Monkeysuits I furnish.

Batteries of ad men
Marching arm in arm
Thru the pages
Of Time & Life

## 23RD CHORUS

The halls of M C A

Singing Deans
In the college morning
Preferable to dry cereal
When no corn mush

Cops & triggers
Magazine pricks
  Dastardly Shadows
And Phantom Hero ines.

Swing yr umbrella
 At the sidewalk
 As you pass
 Or tap a boy
   On the shoulder
   Saying "I say
   Where is Threadneedle
                Street?"

## 24TH CHORUS

San Francisco is too sad
Time, I cant understand
Fog, shrouds the hills in
Makes unshod feet so cold
Fills black rooms with day
  Dayblack in the white windows
  And gloom in the pain of pianos:
Shadows in the jazz age
  Filing by; ladders of flappers
  Painters' white bucket
  Funny 3 Stooge Comedies
    And fuzzy headed Hero
    Moofle Lip suckt it all up
    And wondered why
    The milk & cream of heaven
      Was writ in gold leaf
      On a book—big eyes
      For the world
        The better to see—

## 25TH CHORUS

And big lips for the word
And Buddhahood
And death.
  Touch the cup to these sad lips
Let the purple grape foam
In my gullet deep
 Spread saccharine
  And crimson carnadine
  In my vine of veins
 And shoot power
  To my hand
    Belly heart & head—
      This Magic Carpet
        Arabian World
        Will take us
          Easeful Zinging
        Cross the Sky
        Singing Madrigals

## 26TH CHORUS

To horizons of golden
Moment emptiness
Whither whence uncaring
Dizzy ride in space
To red fires
Beyond the pale,
Rosy gory outlooks
Everywhere.

San Francisco is too old
Her chimnies lean
And look sooty
After all this time
Of waiting for something
To happen
Betwixt hill & house—
Heart & heaven.

## 27TH CHORUS

San Francisco
San Francisco
You're a muttering bum
  In a brown beat suit
  Cant make a woman
  On a rainy corner

Your corners open out
San Francisco
To arc racks
Of the Seals
  Lost in vapors
  Cold and bleak.

## 28TH CHORUS

You're as useless
As a soda truck
Parked in the rain
With cases of pretty red
  Orange green & Coca Cola
    Brown receiving rain
  Drops like the sea
    Receiveth driving spikes
Welling in the navel void.

I also have loud poems:
Broken plastic coverlets
  Flapping in the rain
    To cover newspapers
    All printed up
      And plain.

## 29TH CHORUS

Guys with big pockets
In heavy topcoats
And slit scar
Head bands down
The middle of their hair
All Bruce Barton combed
  Stand surveying Harrison
  Folsom & the Ramp
    And the redbrick clock
  Wishin they had a woman
  Or some money, honey

Westinghouse Elevators
Are full of pretty girls
With classy cans
  And cute pans
  And long slim legs
  And eyes for the boss
  At quarter of four.

## 30TH CHORUS

Old Age is an Indian
With gray hair
And a cane
In an old coat
 Tapping along
 The rainy street
  To see the pretty oranges
 And the stores
  On his big day
When the dog's let out.

Somewhere in this snow
I see little children raped
By maniacal sex fiends
Eager to make a break
But the F B I
In the form of Ted
 Stands waiting
  Hand on gun
 In the Paranoiac
  Summer time
  To come.

## 31ST CHORUS

I knew an angel
In Mexico City
Call'd La Negra
Who the Same eyes
Had as Sebastian
And was reincarnated
To suffer in the poker
House rain
Who had the same eyes
As Sebastian
When his Nirvana came

Sambati was his name.

Must have had one leg once
And expensive armpit canes
And traveled in this rain
With youthful hidden pain

## 32ND CHORUS

Beautiful girls
  Just primp
    But beautiful boys
    Do suffer.

White wash rain stain
Gravel roof glass black
  Red wood blue neon
  Green elevators
  Birds that change color
  And white ants
    Climbing to your knee
      Earnest for deliverance.

## 33RD CHORUS

It was a mournful day
The B O Bay was gray
Old man angry-necks
Stomped to escape sex
And find his Television
In the uptown vision
 Of the milk & secret
   Blossom curtain
   Creak it.

Cheese it the cops!
Ram down the lamb!
  700 Camels
  In Pakistan!

Milk will curdle, honey,
If you sit on stony penises
Three times moving up & down
And 7 times around

## 34TH CHORUS

While young boys peek
In the Hindu temple window
To grow
And come
To A-mer-ri-kay
And be long silent types
In the night clerk cage
Waiting for railroad calls
And hints from Pakistan
Beluchistan and Mien Mo
That Mahatmas
Havent left the field
And tinkle bells
And cobra flutes
Still haunt our campfires
In the calm & peaceful
Night—
Stars of India

## 35TH CHORUS

And speak bashfully
Thru strong brown eyes
Of olden strengths
And bad boy episodes
And a father
With sacred cows
A wandering in his field.
"Rain on, O cloud!"

The taste of worms
Is soft & salty
Like the sea,
Or tears.

And raindrops
That dont know
You've been deceived
Slide on iron
Raggedly gloomy

## 36TH CHORUS

Falling off in wind.

I got the San Francisco
blues
Bluer than misery
I got the San Francisco blues
Bluer than Eternity
I gotta go on home
Fine me
Another
Sanity

I got the San Francisco
blues
Bluer than heaven's gate,
mate,
I got the San Francisco blues
Bluer than blue paint,
Saint,—
I better move on home
Sleep in
My golden
Dream again

## 37TH CHORUS

I got the San Acisca blues
Singin in the street all day
    I got
    The San Acisca
    Blues
Wailin in the street all day
    I better move on, podner,
    Make my West
    The Eastern Way—

San
  Fran
Cis
  Co—
San
  Fran
Cis
    Co
      Oh—
          ba
            by

## 38TH CHORUS

Ever see a tired
    ba by
Cryin to sleep
    in its mother's arms
Wailin all night long
    while the locomotive
Wails on back
A cry for a cry
In the smoke and the lamp
Of the hard ass night

  That's how I
      fee-
          eel—
    That's how
          I fee-eel!
  That's *how*
              I feel—
What a deal!
Yes I'm goin ho
                o
                ome

## 39TH CHORUS

Yes I'm goin
on
home
today

Tonight I'll be ridin
The 80 mile Zipper
And flyin down the Coast
Wrapt in a blanket

Cryin
And cold

So brother
Pour me a drink
I got lots of friends
From coast to coast
And ocean to ocean
girls
But when I see
A bottle a wine
And see that it's full
I like to open it
And take of it my fill

## 40TH CHORUS

And when my head gets dizzy
And friends all laugh
And money pours
    from my pocket
And gold from my ears
And silver flies out
    and rubies explode
I'll up & eat
And sing another song
And drop another grape
  In my belly down

Cause you know
What Omar Khayyam said
  Better be happy
  With the happy grape
  As make long faces
    And groan all night
      In search of fruit
        That dont exist

## 41ST CHORUS

So Mister Engineer
And Mister Hoghead
Conductor Jones
And you head brakeman
And you, tagman
on this run
Give me a hiball
Boomer's or any kind
Start that Diesel
All 3 Units
Less roll on down that rail
See Kansas City by dawn
Or grass of Amarilla
Or rooftops of Old New York
Or banksides green with grass
In April
Anywhere

## 42ND CHORUS

I'd better be a poet
Or lay down dead.

Little boys are angels
Crying in the street
Wear funny hats
Wait for green lights
  Carry bust out tubes
    Around their necks
    And roam the railyards
    Of the great cities
      Looking for locomotives
    Full of shit
      Run down to the waterfront
      And dream of Cathay
      Hook spars with Gulls
        Of athavoid thought.

## 43RD CHORUS

Little Cody Deaver
A San Francisco boy
  Hung by hair of heroes
Growing green & thin
  And soft as sin
  From the tie piles
Of the railer road
  Track where Tokay
  Bottles rust in dust
  Waiting for the term
  Of partiality
  To end up there
    In heaven high
     So's loco can
    Come home
    Con poco coco.

## 44TH CHORUS

Little heroes of the dead
Found a nickle instead
And bought a Borden half & half
  Orange Sherbert & vanil milk
    Trod the pavements
    Of unfall Frisco
    Waiting for its earthquake
  To waver houses men
    And streets to spindle
    Drift to fall at Third
    Street Number 6–15
  Where Bank now stands
  Jack London was born
  And saw gray rigging
  At the 'barcadero
    Pier, His bier
    commemorated in marble
    To advertise the stone
      Of vaults where money rots.

## 45TH CHORUS

Inquisitive plaidshirt
Pops look at trucks
In the afternoon
While Mulligan's
Stewing on the stove
And Calico spreads
  Her milk & creamy legs
  For advertising salesman
    Passing thru from Largo
  Oregon where water
      Runs the Willamette down
      By blasted to-the-North
        Volcanic ashes seft.

## 46TH CHORUS

Babies born screaming
    in this town
Are miserable examples
    of what happens
Everywhere.

Bein Crazy is
The least of my worries.

Now the sun's goin down
In old San Fran
The hills are in a haze
Of Shroudy afternoon—
Bent withered Burroughsian
Greeks pass
In gray felt hats
Expensively pearly
On bony suffer heads

## 47TH CHORUS

And old Indian bo's
With no stockings on
Just Chinese Shuffle
Opium shoes
Take the snaily constitutional
Down 3rd St gray & lost
& Hard to see.

Tragic burpers
With scars of snow
Bound bigly
Huge to find it
To the train
Of time & pain
Waiting at the terminal.

Young punk mankind
Three abreast
Go thriving downwards
In the hellish street.

## 48TH CHORUS

Red shoes of the limpin whore
Who drags her blues
From shore to shore
Along the stores
Lookin for a millioinaire
For her time's up
And she got no guts
And the man aint comin
And I'm no where.

He aint done nothin
But change hats
And go to work
And light a new cigar
And stands in doorway
Swingin the 8 inch
Stogie all around
Arc ing to see
Mankind's vast

## 49TH CHORUS

Sea restless crown
Come rolling bit by bit
  From offices of gloom
  To homes of mortuary
  Hidden Television
  Behind the horse's
    Clock in Hopalong
    The Burper's bestfriend
      Ten gat waving
      Far from children
      Sadly waving
      From the balcony
      Above this street
    Where Acme Paper
          Torn & Tattered
  S'down the parade
  Thrown to clebrate
  McParity's return:

## 50TH CHORUS

All ties in
Like anacin.

Well
So unlock the door
And go to supper
And let the women cook it,
Light's on the hill
The guitar's a-started
Playing by itself
The shower of heaven notes
Plucked by a gypsy woman
In some old dream
Will bless it all
I see furling out
Below—

## 51ST CHORUS

The laundress has bangs
And pursy lips
And thin hips
And sexy walk
And goes much faster
When she knows
The booty in her
laundry bag
Is undiscovered
And unknown
And so no cops watching
she steps on it
t'escape the Feds
of Wannadelancipit
Here in the Standard
Building
Flying High
the
Riding Horse
A Red—

## 52ND CHORUS

None of this means
anything
For krissakes speak up
& be true
Or shut up
& Go to bed

Dead

The wash is waving goodbye
Towards Oakland's russet

I know there are huge clouds
Ballooning beyond the bay

And out Potato Patch,
The snowy sea away,
The milk is furling
Huge and roly
Poly burly puffy

## 53RD CHORUS

Pulsing push
To come on in
Inundate Frisco
 Fill the rills
And ride the ravines
And sneak on in
With Whippoorwill
  To-hoo— To-wa!
    The Chinese call it woo
    The French les brumes
    The British
          Fog
L A
    Smog
Heaven
      Cellar door

## 54TH CHORUS

Communities of houses
Caparisoned by sunlight
On the last & fading hill
Of America a-rollin
    Rollin
To the Western Chill

And delicacies of statues
Hewn by working men
Neoned, tacked on,
Pressed against the sign
    Mincin
    Mincin
To sell the swellest coupon

Understand?

Light on the fronts
    of old buildings
Like in New York
In December dusks
When hats point to sea

## 55TH CHORUS

This means
that everything
has some home
to come to
Light has windows
balconies of iron
like New Orleans

It also has all space
And I have windows
balconies of iron
like New Orleans

I also have all space

And St Louis too

Light follows rivers
I do too

Light fades, I pass

## 56TH CHORUS

Light illuminates
The intense cough
Of young girls in love
Hurrying to sell their
future husband
On the Market St
Parade

Light makes his face
reddern
Her white mask

She sucks to bone him dry
And make him happy
Make him cry
Make him baby
Stay by me.

## 57TH CHORUS

Crooks of Montreal
  Tossing up their lighters
    To a cigarette of snow
    Intending to plot evil
    And break the pool machine
      Tonight off Toohey's head
      And the Frisco fire team
      Come howling round
      The corner of the dream

## 58TH CHORUS

Immense the rivets
In the broadsides
Of battleships
  Fired upon head on
  In face to face combat
  In the Philippines
   Anchored Alameda
   Overtime for toilets
    On Labor Day

## 59TH CHORUS

IL
W
U
Has tough white seamen
Scrapping snow white hats
In favor of iron clubs
To wave in inky newsreels
When Frisco was a drizzle
And Curran all sincere,
Bryson just a baby,
Reuther bloodied up,
—When publications
Of Union pamphleteers
Featured human rock jaws
Jutting Editorialese
Composed by angry funny
redhead editors
Walking with their heads down
To catch the evening fleet
And wave goodbye to sailors
passing rosely dreams
Into a sparkling cannon
Gray & spicked & span
To shine the Admiral
In his South Pacific pan—

## 60TH CHORUS

No such luck
  For Potter McMuck
Who broke his fist
On angry mitts
In fist fights
Falling everywhere
From down Commercial
  To odd or even
All the piers
  Blang! Bang!
  I L W U had a hard time
  And so did N A M
  And S P A M
  And as did A M

## 61ST CHORUS

YOU INULT ME EVERY NIME, MALN BWANO
Ladies and Gentle-man
The phoney woiker
You here see
Got can one time
In Toonisfreu
Ger ma nyeee
Becau he had
no dime
To give the con duck teur
Yo see he stiffled
For his miffle
And couldnt cough a little
Bill de juice ran
down his Sfam.

## 62ND CHORUS

JULIEN LOVE'S SOUND
"All
right!
Here we are
with all the little lambs.
Has anyone disposed
of my old man
Last night?
Mortuary deeds,
Dead,
Drink, me down
Table or two,
Wher'd you put it
Kerouac?
The bottoms in your bag
Of cellar heaven doors
And hellish consistencies
Gelatinous & composed
Will bang & break
Apon the time clock
Beat prow stone bong
Boy
Before I give YOU
An idgit of the
Kind Love Legend"

## 63RD CHORUS

JULIEN LOVE'S JUDGMENT
"Seriously boy
This San Francisco
Blues of yours
Like shark fins
the summer before
And was it Sarie
Sauter Finnegan
Some gal before—
It's a farce
For funny you
you know?
I dont think I'll buy it"

Slit in the ear
By a bolo knife
Savannah Kid just nodded
At the beast that
Hides.

Secret
Poetry
Deceives
Simply

## 64TH CHORUS

California evening is like Mexico
The windows get golden oranges
The tattered awnings flap
Like dresses of old Perdido
  Great Peruvian Princesses
    In the form of Negro Whores
    Go parading down the sidewalk
    Wearing earrings, sweet perfume
      Old Weazel Warret

    tradesmen
     sick of selling
     out their stores stand in
        the evening lineup
        before identifying cops
        they cannot understand
        in the clouds of can
         and iron moosing
         marshly morse
         of over head

## 65TH CHORUS

Daughters of Jerusalem
Prowling like angry felines
Statuesque & youthful
 From the well
 Embarrassed but implacable
 And watched by hungry worriers
  Filling out the whitewall
   Car with 1000 pounds
   Of "Annergy!
    Thats what I got!
   An-nergy!"
  To burn up Popocatepetl's
   Torch of ecstasy.

The neons redly twangle
 Twinkle cute & clean
 Like Millbrae cherry
  Nipptious tostle
   Flowers tattled
   Petal for the joss stick
   Stuck in neon twaddles
   To advertise a bar
 —All over SanFranPisco
  The better is the pain

## 66TH CHORUS

—"Switch to Calvert"
Runs an arrow eating
Bulb by bulb
Across the bulbous
Whisky bottle
And under the Calvert clock

Tastes better! Everyone
Tastes better
All the time

And fieldhands
That aint got aznos
But the same south Mexican
Evening soft shoe
walk
Slow in dusts of soft
in Ac to pan
Here in Frisco City
American
The same way walk
To buy some vegetables

## 67TH CHORUS

For the bedsprings on the roof
  Not keep the rain on out
Or bombed out huts
  In dumpland—Blue
Workjacket, shino pants,
  It's like Mexico all violet
    At ruby rose & velvet
      Sun on down
        On down
    Sun on down
      Sundown

Red blood bon neon
  Bon runs  don  blon

By Barrett
      Wimpole
            Trackmeet

## 68TH CHORUS

And like Mexico the deep
Gigantic scorpic haze
Of shady curtain night
  Bein drawn on civilized
  And Fellaheen will howl
  Where the cows of mush
Rush to hide their sad
  Tan hides in the stonecrump
  Mumps bump top of hill
    Out Mission Way
    Holy Cows of Cross
    And Lick Monastery

        Velvet for our meat
        Hamburgers

  And doom of pained nuns
    Or painted
          One
    Mexico is like Universe

## 69TH CHORUS

And Third Street a Sun
Showing just how's done
The light the life the action
The limp of worried reachers
Crawling up the Cuba street
In almost dark
To find the soften bell
Creaming Meek on corner
One by one, Tem, Tim,
Click, gra, rattapisp,
Ting, Tang—

Blink! Off
Run! Arrow!
Cut! Winkle! Twinkle!
Fill
Piss! Pot!
The lights of coldmilk
supper hill streets
make me davenport
and cancel Ship.

## 70TH CHORUS

3rd St is like Moody St
Lowell Massachusetts
It has Bagdad blue
Dusk down sky
And hills with lights
And pale the hazel
Gentle blue in the
burned windows
Of wooden tenements,
And lights of bars,
music brawl,
"Hoap!" "Hap!" & "Hi"
In the street of blood
And bells billygoating
Boom by at the ache
of day
The break of personalities
Crossing just once
In the wrong door

## 71ST CHORUS

Nevermore to remain
Nevermore to return
—The same hot hungry
harried hotel
wild Charlies dozzling
to fold the
Food papers in the
mahogany talk
Of television reading room
Balls are walled
and withered
and long fergit.

Moody Lowell Third Street
Sick & tired bedsprings
Silhouettes of brownlace
eve night dowse—
All that—
And outsida town
The aching snake
Pronging underground
To come eat up
Us the innocent
And insincere in here

## 72ND CHORUS

And Budapest Counts
Driving lonely mtn. cars
On the hem of the grade
Of the lip curve hill
Where Rockly meets
Out Market & More—
The last shore—
View of the sea
Seal

Only Lowell has for sea
The imitative Merrimac

And Frisco has for
snake
The crowdy earthquake
cataract
And Hydrogen Bombs
of Hope
Lost in the blue
Pacific
Empty sea

## 73RD CHORUS

Bakeries gladly bright
Filled with dour girls
Buying golden pies
For sullen brooding boys

On 3rd St in the night

But by day
  The Greek Armenian
    Milk of honey
  Bee baclava maker
  Puts his sugars
  On the counter
    For bums with avid jaws
  And hollow eyes
    Eager to eat
    Their last dainty.

## 74TH CHORUS

Marchesa Casati
Is a living doll
Pinned on my Frisco
Skid row wall

Her eyes are vast
Her skin is shiny
Blue veins
And wild red hair
Shoulders sweet & tiny

Love her
Love her
Sings the sea
Bluely
Moaning
In the Augustus John
de John
back ground.

## 75TH CHORUS

Her eyes are living dangers
'll Leap you
From a page
Wearing the same insanity
The sweet unconcernedly
Italian humanity
Glaring from black eyebrows
To ask
Of Renaissance:
"What have you done now
After 3 hundred years
But create the glary witness
Which out this window
Shows a pale green
Friscan hill
The last green hill
Of America
With a cut a band

## 76TH CHORUS

Of brown red road
Coint round
By architects of hiways
To show the view
To ledge travellers
Of Frisco, City, Bay
And Sea
As all you do is drive around
—By Groves of lonesome
Redwood trees
Isolated
In physical isolation
On the bare lump
Hill like people
Of this country
Who walk alone
In streets all day
Forbidden
To contact physically
Anybody
So desirable—

## 77TH CHORUS

They kill'd all painters
Drown'd—Made wash
The smothering crone
Of Cathay,
  Flower of Malaya,
  And Dharma saws,
  Gat it all in,
    Like wash,
    Call'd it Renascence
    And then wearied
      From the globe—
        Hill, last hill
        Of Western World
          Is cut around
          Like half attempted
          Half castrated
          Protrudient breast
            Of milk
          From wild staring earth

## 78TH CHORUS

—The last scar
America was able
  To create
  The uttermost hill
  Beyond which is just
        Pacific
  And no more sc-cuts
  And Alamos neither
  But that can be rolled
  In satisfying sea
  Absolved of suicide—
    Except that now
    They're blasting fishermen
      Apart?"

## 79TH CHORUS

"Beyond that fruitless sea"
—So speaks Marchesa
Mourning the Renaissance
And still the breeze
Is sweet & soft
 And cool as breasts
 And wild as sweet dark eyes.

Sits in her spirit
Like she wont be long
And bright about it
  All the time, like short
      star

    An angry proud beauty
    Of Italy

## 80TH CHORUS

San Francisco Blues
Written in a rocking chair
In the Cameo Hotel
San Francisco Skid row
Nineteen Fifty Four.

This pretty white city
On the other side of the country
Will no longer be
Available to me
I saw heaven move
Said "This is the End"
Because I was tired
of all that portend.

And any time you need
me
Call
I'll be at the other
end
Waiting
at the final hall

# RICHMOND HILL BLUES

DULUOZ
Name derived from early
morning sources
In a newspaper office
Long Ago in Lowell Mass
When birds were shitting
On the canal
And Sperm was Floating
among the Redbrick Walls
Of a Morn that had Smoke
Pouring from a Christian Hill
Chimney—
Ah Sire, Duluoz,
King of my Thoughts,
Salute!
(Kick another can of beer)

THAT'S WHAT I SAID
Not what I thot I meant
O Sin-of-a-Bitch
But what I out loud said
Not—again—what in
retrospect
And banalizing sedeora ing
of my garage
Made it
Say what you mean
A poem is a lark
A pie

SCHLITZ (A drunken vision of a can of beer)
Beaded melt hotwave waters
Of outside hydrated juices
Flowing down Made in USA
& Brooklyn New York
Genuine, holed triangular.

WIFE & 3

Little Cathy gladdy
  with sun cheeks
  beeted
Jamie hiding hugging
  her knees
Mother Earwicker solemn,
    lovely, flesh legs
    white
King John Fartitures
  of Hop Top Heap
  Cassadee-ing in
  his Kingdom
Jamie of mother's sweetly
  sweet goodheart breast
Showing oldlady teeth
    of littlegirl glee
 And pudgy arms locked

Tristesse in the little
  hopeless Fingers,
Faisse in the shot,
    the radiant sun,
The shine of San Jose
O
  Grass
          Peotés of time!

    Steps, lost davenports,
      eternities,
Hot Night Birds,
    Billy Holiday!
—Make the quaker
  give his cream

ANY TIME

Any time you want
A write a fucken poem
Ope this book
& Scream no more
But Cream
Cry
Fret not
  Flow
  Flay
  Fray the edge of Froy
Make Frogs Alliterate
    Bekkek! Bekkek!
      Koak! Koak!
      Carra Quax!
      Carra qualquus
          Kerouacainius!

EVEN JOYCE

Even he, Joyce,
    had love—
Even blind poets

AUDEN HAD NO ASS

Auden had no ass
Butler had no balls
Carew had no crash
Dyck had no dick
Egrets had no erse
Fart had no fuck
George had no Gyzm
His honou had no H
I J Fox had no wife
J Fox had no Joke
Kerou had no Ka
Ling Woe had no Rice
M & N had no Moola
(a lot!)
Novales had no Nodes
O vum had no Ollie
(O'Neill Mc Shanahan)
P-ew had no Push
Quasi Quean had no Queasy
feelings
R had no heart
Studentio
had
no
Stok
To
v
e
l
e
n
l
s

h had
no

T
u
p

Uvalde had no Upstarts
Vedichad no Velda
Velda had no Vim

Vish had no Rush
her
Vim
hid
his
Or pit his ass
gainst my pen

U had no V
V had no Victory
U V W had no
Pesco
X no Y or Z

THE POET
So many times since
I've seen the poet
of Greenwich Village
Cutting to work in the gray dawn
With a lunchpail &
    bleak haircut
  Eyes to the Hudson
    Nostril to the street
    To winter, work, beneficence,
Meals, fare of folly
So many times since
I've seen the poet
Who wrote rhythms & rhymes
To be mad in Minetta's
And Minetta Lane
  Go Hurrying to Work
  Sex hung, sexed, psycho-
      analyzed?
To work in the unpoetic dawn

Mornings after I'd got drunk
with Lucien & Allen
    & Allied Angels
In the Vast Manhattan
      Fish—
O America!
  Songs!
  Poems!
    Altos!  Tenors!
        Blow!
(Poet is Dead)

THUNDER

Thunder makes a booming
noise like windows
Being hysterically quietly
closed—
So Papa fell down the stairs
of time
In spite of holy water
And all yr mixed drinks
in
Eternity

EMILY DICKINSON

Ere so sober Emily
  Did New England sow
  With brooms of activity
  I'd the tree-rock spoken to.
But it only said to me
"This sleet's crack
  You hear cracking my hide
  Is the voice of olden poets
  Not far from rocks of here
  Did their olden eyes
  On nature bestow blue
  —" I said
"Ah Oh How So Sad."

I said—"And graves?"
And I said "Darling
Supposing it should
  To nature
  Suddenly occur
  To make unending poets
  Unendingly Blow"

Nature Said: "Mean,
  I dont know what you
Mean"—
"Ah Nature, Ah Rock,"
I cried, "Nobody's Bone
 Has so suffusèd been,
 No burden of boredom
 Greater
 No love colder
 No love life less
 No grave nearer
 Always
 Than Ye Bard"

ROSE

"Ah Rose," I cried,
"Shine in the Phosphorescent
Night."

BUG

And to the little bug which am myself
I said
"Bug, lip, tip, tit of time,
Try, take, take, flake, fly,
Love is passing yr. cheekbones
On the phosphorescent transparent
wing
Of Kafka's cheese consuming
Metamorphosed Bug"

HORROR

So then I saw horror,
And I cried,
"Horrer, leave me er lone."
Horrer-horror laid me bone
By bone in a bag of dirt,
I was broiled in the oven
Of heaven in the silver foil
Of Devil Jesus God
Which is Yr Holy Trinity

---

SMILES

Smiles pull flesh from cheek
Over pearls of bone
  And make the watcher see
  The quake of cream
  In eyes of stone

ON TEARS

Tears is the break of my brow,
The moony tempestuous
    sitting down
In dark railyards
When to see my mother's face
Recalling from the waking vision
I wept to understand
The trap mortality
And personal blood of earth
Which saw me in—
  Father father
  Why hast thou forsaken me?
Mortality & unpleasure
Roam this city—
Unhappiness my middle name
  I want to be saved,—
  Sunk—can't be
  Won't be
  Never was made to—
  So retch!

WHEN OLD

When I began to grow old
And could feel my left arm
numben
And brain resisted hope,
Will sat sleeping
Energy thubbd exhausted
in my eye
And love fled me—
When the worst news
Was brought to me
And I exulted to be alone
Go die
I had a vision of
the saint
Misunderstood & too tired
to explain why
And sweet intentioned
in another day—
Even Stanley Gould'll
go to heaven

BOP

Sweet little dop a la pee—
Bit bit piano tip
tinkle plips
And smash prop brushes
In the little numb moment
um

I KNOW

I know that I cannot write
verse
But this is my beercan short
line
Book so bear with me
invisible
Reader and let me goof
even
When I'm sick & have no
ideas

GOD

Sitting over our meanings
Egomaniac God,
Lonely slick & rain glint
Also uses irritating us
In the Real.

HOPES

Poetry doesnt know:
The air conditioner
Not in use in winter
Is like my hopes—
Half in, half out,
Green on a whitewall,
S'only good to cast
A long shadow
In the bleak street light

TREE

But a tree has
    a living suffering shape
Is spread in half
  by 2 limbed fate
Rises from gray rain
    pavements
To traffic in the bleak
    brown air
Of cities radar television
    nameless dumb &
    numb mis connicumb
  Throwing twigs the
        color of ink
  To white souled
        heaven, with
  A reality of its own uses

TENORMAN

Sweet sad young tenor
Horn slumped around neck
Bearded full of junk
Slouches waiting
For Apocalypse,
Listens to the new
Negro raw trumpet kid
Tell him the wooden news;
And the beat of the bass
The bass—drives in
Drummer drops a bomb
Piano tinkle tackles
Sweet tenor lifting
All American sorrows
Raises mouthpiece to mouth
And blows to finger
  The iron sounds

# BOWERY BLUES

For I
Prophesy
That the night
Will be bright
With the gold
Of old
In the inn
Within.

Cooper Union Cafeteria—late cold March afternoon, the street (Third Avenue) is cobbled, cold, desolate with trolley tracks—Some man on the corner is waving his hand down No-ing somebody emphatically and out of sight behind a black and white pillar, cold clowns in the moment horror of the world—A Porto Rican kid with a green stick, stooping to bat the sidewalk but changing his mind and halting on—Two new small trucks parked—The withery grey rose stone building across the street with its rime heights in the quiet winter sky, inside are quiet workers by neon entablatures practicing fanning lessons with the murderous Marbo—A yakking blonde with awful wide smile is makking her mouth lip talk to an old Bodhisattva papa on the sidewalk, the tense quickness of her hard working words—Meanwhile a funny bum with no sense trys to panhandle them and is waved away stumbling, he doesnt care about society women embarrassed with paper bags on sidewalks—Unutterably sad the broken winter shattered face of a man passing in the bleak ripple—Followed by a Russian boxer with an expression of Baltic lostness, something grim and Slavic and so helplessly beyond my conditional ken or ability to evaluate and believe that I shudder as at the touch of cold stone to think of him, the sickened old awfulness of it like slats of wood wall in an old brewery truck

Shin Mc Ontario with
no money, no bets, no
health, pauls on by
pawing his inside coat
no hope of ever
seeing Miami again
since he lost his pickles
on Orchard Street
and his father
S t u h t e l f e d e h r e d
him to hospitals
Of gray
bleak
bone
drying
in the moon
that mortifies his coat
and words sing
what mind
brings

Bleeding bloody seamen
Of Indian England
Battering in coats
Of Third Ave noo
With no sense and their brows
Streaked with wine sop
Blood of ogligit
Sad adventurers
Far from the pipe
Of Liverpool
The bean of bone
Bottle Liffey brown
Far hung unseen
Top tippers
Of o cean wave.

God bless & sing for them
As I  can not

*

Cooper Union Blues,
The Musak is too Sod.
The gayety of grave
Candidates makes
My gut weep
And my brains
Are awash
Down the side of the
        blue orange table
As little sneery snirfling
Porto Rican hero
Ba t ts by booming
His coat pocket
Fisting to the Vicinity
Where Mortuary
Waits for bait.
(What kind of service
Do broken barrels give?)
    O have pity
      Bodhisattva
      Of Intellectual
      Ra  diance!

Save the world from her eyebrows
Of beautiful illusion
Hope, O hope,
O Nope, O pope

———

Crowded coat ers
In a front seat

Car, gray & grim,
Push on thru
To the basketball

*

Various absurd parades—
The strict in tact
Intent man with
Broken back
Balling his suitcase
Down from Washington
Building in the night
Passing little scaggly
Childreyn with Ma's
Of mopey hope.

———

Too sad, too sad
The well kept
Clean cut
Ferret man.

*

And the old blue Irishman
With untenable dignity
Beer bellying home
To drowsy dowdy TV
Suppers of gravy
And bile—
Wearing old new coats
Meant to be smooth on youths
Wrinkled on his barrel
Like sea wind
Infatuating sea eyes

To thinkin
Ripples & old age
Are real.

*

Poor young husbandry
  With coat of tan
Digging change in palms
  For bleaker coffees
Than afternoon gloom
  Where work of stone
Was endowed
   With tired hope.
Hope  O hope
Cooper Union Hope
O Bowery of Hopes!
O absence!
O blittering real
Non staring redfaced
Wild reality!
Hiding in the night
Like my dead father
I see the crystal
Shavings shifting
Out of sight
Dropping pigeons of light
To the Turd World
Enought, sad ones—
False petals
Of pure lotus
In drugstore windows
Where cups of O
Are smoked

Paddy Mc Gilligan
Muttering in the street

Just hit town
From C a l c i  bleak

Ole Mop Polock Pat
Angry as a cat
About to stumble
Into the movie
Of the night
Through which he sees
M  oo  da  lands
Un seen
Like waking in the night
To transcendental Milk
In the room

---

Sad Jewish respectable
rag men with trucks
And watchers
Shaking cloth
Into the gutter
Saying  I dunno, no, no,
As gray green hat
Sits on their heads
Protecting them
From Infinity above
Which shines with white
Wide & brown black clouds
As Liberty Sun
Honks over the Sea
Sending Ships
From inner sea
Free
To de rool york
Pock Town of Part
Shelf High Hawk

Man Dung Town.
Rinkidink Charley is Crazy.

*

Ugly pig
Burping
In the sidewalk
As surrealistic
Typewriters
Swim exploding by
And bigger marines
Lizard thru the side
Of the gloom
Like water
For this
is the Sea
Of
Reality.

*

The story of man
Makes me sick
Inside, outside,
I dont know why
Something so conditional
And all talk
Should hurt me so.

I am hurt
I am scared
I want to live
I want to die
I dont know
Where to turn
In the Void

And when
To cut
Out

---

For no Church told me
No Guru holds me
No advice
Just stone
Of New York
And on the cafeteria
We hear
The saxophone
Of dead Ruby
Died of Shot
In Thirty Two,
Sounding like old times
And de bombed
Empty decapitated
Murder by the clock.
And I see Shadows
Dancing into Doom
In love, holding
Tight the lovely asses
Of the little girls
In love with sex
Showing themselves
In white undergarments
At elevated windows
Hoping for the Worst.

I cant take it
Anymore
If I cant hold
My little behind
To me in my room

Then it's goodbye
Sangsara
For me
Besides
Girls arent as good
As they look
And Samadhi
Is better
Than you think
When it stars in
Hitting your head
In with Buzz
Of glittergold
Heaven's Angels
Wailing
Saying
We ve been waiting for you
  Since Morning, Jack
—Why were you so long
  Dallying in the sooty room?
  This Transcendental Brilliance
  Is the better part
  (Of Nothingness
  I sing)

Okay.
Quit.
Mad.
Stop.

———

# MACDOUGAL STREET BLUES

## IN THE FORM OF 3 CANTOS

*

## CANTO UNO

The goofy foolish
human parade
Passing on Sunday
art streets
Of Greenwich Village

Pitiful drawings of
images on an
iron fence
ranged there
by selfbelieving
artists
with no hair
and black berets
showing green seas
eating at rock
and Pleiades
of Time

Pestiferating at moon squid
Salt flat tip fly toe
tat sand traps
With cigar smoking interesteds
puffing at the
stroll

I mean sincerely
  naive sailors buying prints
Women with red banjos
   On their handbags
   And arts handicrafty
   Slow shuffling
   art-ers of Washington Sq
    Passing in what they think
   Is a happy June afternoon
Good God the Sorrow
  They dont even listen to me when
  I try to tell them they will die

They say "Of course I know
I'll die, why should you mention
It now—Why should I worry
About it—it'll happen
  It'll happen—Now
  I want a good time—
  Excuse me—
  It's a beautiful happy June
  Afternoon I want to walk in—

Why are you so tragic & gloomy?"
And on the corner at the
      Pony Stables
Of Sixth Ave & 4th
Sits Bodhisattva Meditating
In Hobo Rags
 Praying at Joe Gould's chair
For the Emancipation

Of the shufflers passing by,
Immovable in Meditation
He offers his hand & feet
  To the passers by
And nobody believes

That there's nothing to believe in.
Listen to Me.
There is no sidewalk artshow
No strollers are there

No poem here, no June
afternoon of Oh
But only Imagelessness
Unrepresented on the iron fence
Of bald artists
With black berets
Passing by
One moment less than this
Is future Nothingness Already

The Chess men are silent, assembling
Ready for funny war—
Voices of Washington Sq Blues
Rise to my Bodhisattva Poem
Window
I will describe them:
E y t k e y ee
S a l a o s o
F r u p t u r t

Etc.
No need, no words to
describe
The sound of Ignorance—
They are strolling to
their death
Watching the Pictures of Hell
Eating Ice Cream
of Ignorance
On wood sticks

That were once sincere
in trees—
But I cant write, poetry,
just prose

I mean
This is prose
Not poetry
But I want
To be sincere

## CANTO DOS

While overhead is the perfect blue
    emptiness of the sky
  With its imaginary balloons
        of false sight
  Flying around in it
        like Tathagata Flying Saucers
  These poor ignorant things
        mill on sidewalks
  Looking at pitiful pictures
          of what they think

Is reality
And one
    a Negro with curls
Even has a camera
    to photograph
The pictures
And Jelly Roll Man
Pops his Billy Bell
  Good Humor for Sale—
W Somerset Maugham
          is on my bed

An ignorant storyteller
    millionaire queer
But Ezra Pound
    he crazy—
As the perfect sky
    beginninglessly pure
Thinglessly perfect
    waits already
They pass in multiplicity

Parading among Images
Images Images Looking
Looking—
And everybody's turning around
& pointing—
Nobody looks up
and In
Nor listens to Samantabhadra's
Unceasing Compassion

No Sound Still
S s s s t t
Seethe
Of Sea Blue Moon
Holy X-Jack
Miracle
Night—
Instead, yank & yucker
For pits & pops

Look for crashes
Pictures
Squares
Explosions
Birth
Death
Legs
I know, sweet hero,
Enlightenment has Come
Rest in Still

In the Sun Think
Think Not
Think no more Lines—
Straw hat, hands aback
Classed

He exam in a tein distinct
Rome prints—
Trees prurp
and saw—

The Chessplayers Wont End
Still they sit
Millions of hats
In underwater foliage
Over marble games
The Greeks of Chess
Plot the Pop
of Mate
King Queen

—I know their game,
their elephant with the pillar
With the pearl in it,
their gory bishops
And Vital Pawns—
Their devout frontline
Sacrificial pawn shops
Their Stately king

Who is so tall
Their Virgin Queen
Pree ing to Knave
the Night Knot
—Their Bhagavad Gitas
of Ignorance,
Krishna's advice,

Comma,
The game begins—
But hidden Buddha
Nowhere to be seen
But everywhere

In air atoms
In balloon atoms
In imaginary sight atoms
In people atoms

In people atoms
Again
In image atoms
In me & you atoms
In atom bone atoms
Like the sky
Already waits
For us eyes open to
—Pawn fell

Horse reared
Mate Kiked Cattle
And Boom! Cop
shot Bates—
Cru put Two—
Out—I cried—
Pound Pomed—
Jean-Louis,
Go home, Man.

I mean.—
As solid as anything
Is this reality of images
In the imageless essence,
Neither of em'll quit
—So tho I am wise
I have to wait like
anyotherfool

## CANTO TRES

Lets forget the strollers
  Forget the scene
Lets close our eyes
  Let me Instruct Thee
    Here is dark milk
    Here is our Sweet Mahameru
      Who will Coo
      To You Too

As he did to me
One night at three
When I w k e l t
      P l e e
  knelt to See
  Realit ee
    And I said
  'Wilt thou protect me
      for ' ver ?'

And he in his throatless
    deep mother hole
  Replied 'H  o  m'
  (Pauvre Ange)
  Mahameru
    Tathagata of Mercy
See
  He
    Now
      in dark escrow

  In the middleless dark
of eyelids' lash obliviso
  so
  Among rains of Transcendent
      Pity

Abides since Ever
Before Evermore ness
of Thusness Imagined
O Maha Meru

O Mountain Sumeru
O Mountain of Gold
O Holy Gold
O Room of Gold
O Sweet peace
rememberance
O Navalit Yuku

Of sweet cactus
Thorn of No Time
—Ply me onward
like boat
thru this Sea
Safe to Shore
Ulysses never Sore
—Bless me Gerard
Bless thee, Living

I shall pray for all
sentient human
& otherwise sentient
beings here & everywhere
now—

No names
Not even faces
One Pity
One Milk
One Lovelight
s a v e

*

# DESOLATION BLUES

## IN 12 CHORUSES

### 1ST CHORUS

I stand on my head on Desolation Peak
And see that the world is hanging
Into an ocean of endless space
The mountains dripping rock by rock
Like bubbles in the void
And tending where they want—
That at night the shooting stars
Are swimming up to meet us
Yearning from the bottom black
  But never make it, alas—
  That we walk around clung
  To earth
  Like beetles with big brains
Ignorant of where we are, how,
What, & upsidedown like fools,
  Talking of governments & history,
—But Mount Hozomeen
The most beautiful mountain I ever seen,
Does nothing but sit & be a mountain,
A mess of double pointed rock
Hanging pouring into space
  O frightful silent endless space
—Everything goes to the head
  Of the hanging bubble, with men
  The juice is in the head—
  So mountain peaks are points
  Of rocky liquid yearning

## 2ND CHORUS

Mountains have skin, said Peter
    Orlovsky of San Francisco—
And gorges shoot up clouds of mist
  That look like planet smoke—
Dead trees, artistic as a cottage
    on Truro,
  Look like goat horns off a rock,
—Alpine firs turn evergreen browns
By August First when summer's dead
At high elevations—the creeks roar
  And cataracts tumble pouring
  But it's all upsidedown & strange
—Why do I sit here crosslegged
On this steaming rocky surface
Of a planet called earth
Scribbling with a pencil
Unmusical songs called songs
And why worry my juicy head
And rail my bony hand at words
  And look around for more
    And nothing means nothing
      as of yore?—
  T  s the primordial essence
  Manifesting forms, of happy
  And unhappy, stuff & no-stuff,
    Matter & space, phenomena
    Front & noumena behind,
    Out of exuberant nothingness

## 3RD CHORUS

Yet birds mumble in the morning,
And raccoons tumble down the draws,
  I saw one hit by his own rock
  In a lil raccoon avalankey—
  And firs point as ever
                to infinity,
Their fine points top points too,
—Birds squeak like mice,
  and moonlight bucks & does
Graze in my yard like cows
With big shootable flanks,
  And hooves of eternity, clatter
    on the rocks,
  Run away when I open the door,
  Down the hill, like silly frightened
    schoolteachers—
Chipmunks are well named—
Bears & abominable snowmen
I have not yet seen—
    Proud a that line—
Rock slides take generations to form,
  I try to rush it along—
  No rain in a month, nor yet
    a month, within a month—
  The beaked furthereal pine
    points at a crazy
  Upsidedown mid morning moon
    as delicate
  As a slide, like snow

## 4TH CHORUS

All the worries that've plagued
everybody since Moses, Homer,
Sappho, Uparli, Cannibals and
Patawatamkonalokunopuh
Are worrin and playin me
on this mount of mystery—
I've T S Elioted all the fogs,
Faulknered all the stone,
Balanced nothing gainst something,
played solitaire, smoked,
Brought bashing sticks to midnight
frightful long tailed rats
And ranted at mosquitos,
And remembered my mother
her sweet labors of home
And the cold eyed sister
who made a bum outa me,
And friends, & goodtimes,
& prayed & gave up prayer,
And pondered history, myths,
stories, artistic plans, plays,
French movies, phalanxes
of disordered human crazy
Thought, & still it's upsidedown—
Silent—stiff—wont yield—
Wont tell—A big empty
Puppet stage, with rock

## 5TH CHORUS

Distant valleys in Canada
look like they'd beckon
but I know better,—
I yearn for the flatlands again,
the gentle hill,—
At 4 PM the clouds of hope
Are horizon salmon floaters
Full of strange promise
abstracted from the golden age
in my breast—
Patches of snow dont do anything
but be
Patches of snow, till they melt,
And then water, it's nothing
but water
Till sun evaporates, then mist,
It's (as I look) nothing but mist
As it rises ululatory responding
to every shift of wind,
And will be mist, and will be
Mist,
And ants are nothing but just
ants,
And rocks'll sit where they are
forever
Lessn I move em, throw em
down the gorge,
And then they spit a minute

## 6TH CHORUS

I just dont understand—
tho mist'll be mist till
Heavens obdure, tho man'll
Be man till heavens obdure
Or hells obscure I just
dont
I just dont
Dont
Understand
I dont—
I want to know—soon's a do
I dont understand—if I said:
"I dont care" I understand—
I understand that
it doesnt matter.
Still the birdy clings, to earth,
He dont go silent on me,
I dont stop writing,
I dont stop living,
What a fool,—bust the bird.
The only thing that ever happens
to Hozomeen
Is that he'll get a wreath
of clouds
Every now & then
& breed to revel
Without moving a mighty shoulder
—I envy him his rock

## 7TH CHORUS

But I want to live, I want
    to get down
Off this Chinese Han Shan hill
    and make it
To the city & walk the streets
And drink good wine
    (Christian Brothers Port)
Or whiskey (Early Times
        or Old Grand Dad)
  And go to Chinese Movies
        on Saturday Afternoon
  And buy presents in the window
  and watch the dust gather
  On little stationary toys
  In celluloid windows of children
And go to the vast markets
  And eat tortillas beans
        ice cream
  And crime—and banana splits
        and tea
  And benzedrine & broads—
        and waterfronts
  And plays & play marquees
        and Square Times
  And you—I'd like to celebrate
        upside
    Down in cities

## 8TH CHORUS

Once I saw a giant
in a building

He's here now, bending
over me,
Giant diamond gone insane.
Ta, the Golden Eternity,
Ta Ta Ta Ta,
Tathata, trumpet, Ta Ta,
This giant diamond might
Here is got some name'r other
But *I dont know*
*I dont care*
*and it makes no difference*
And now I'm wise.
When the whole wide world
is fast asleep I cry.
Let me offer you
my reassuring profile
Saying, "It's okay, girl, we'll
make it
Till the sun goes down forever
And until then what you got
to lose
But the losing? We're fallen
angels
Who didnt believe
That nothing means nothing."

## 9TH CHORUS

We're hanging into the abyss
of blue—
In it is nothing but innumerable
and endless worlds
More numerous even (& the number
of beings!)
Than all the rocks that cracked
And became little rocks
In all that rib of rock
That extends from Alaska,
Nay the Aleutian tips,
Down through these High Cascades,
Through to California & Ensenada,
Down, through High Tepic, down
To Tehuantepec, down,
The rib, to Guatemala & on,
Colombia, Andes, till the High
Bottom Chilean & Tierra
del Fuego
O yoi yoi
And on around to Siberia—
In other words, & all the grains
of sand that comprise
A rock, and all the grains
of atomstuff therein,
More worlds than that
in the empty blue sea
We hang in, upsidedown,
—Too much to be real

## 10TH CHORUS

But it's real
it's as real as the squares
on this page
And as real as my sore ass
sitting on a rock
And as real as hand, sun,
pencil, knee,
Ant, breezed, stick,
water, tree, color,
peeop, birdfeather,
snag, smoke,
haze, goat,
appearance
and low crazed cloud
And dream of the Far Northwest
And the little mounted policeman
Of my dreams on a ridge—
Not an Indian in sight—
Real, real as fog in London town
and croissants in Paris
and swchernepetchzels
in Prienna
And Praha Maha Fuckit
—Real, real,
unreal,
deal,
Zeal,
I say, dont care if it's real
or unreal, I'se

## 11TH CHORUS

And if you dont like the tone
of my poems
You can go jump in the lake.
I have been empowered
to lay my hand
On your shoulder
and remind you
That you are utterly free,
Free as empty space.
You dont have to be famous,
dont have to be perfect,
Dont have to work,
dont have to marry,
Dont have to carry burdens,
dont have to gnaw & kneel,

the taste
of rain—
Why kneel?

Dont even have to sit,
Hozomeen,
Like an endless rock camp
go ahead & blow,

Explode & go,
I wont say nothin,
neither this rock,
And my outhouse doesnt care,
And I got no body

## 12TH CHORUS

Little weird flower,
why did you grow?
Who planted you
on this god damned hill?
Who asked you to grow?
Why dont you go?
What's wrong with yr. orange tips?
I was under the impression
that you were sposed to be
some kind of perfect nature.
Oh, you are?
Just jiggle in the wind. I see.
At yr feet I see a nosegay
bou kay
Of seven little purple apes
who dint grow so high
And a sister of yours
further down the precipice—
and your whole family
to the left—
I thot last week
you were funeral bouquets
for me
that never askt
to be born
or die
But now I guess
I'm just talkin
thru my
empty head

# ORIZABA 210 BLUES

## 1ST CHORUS

Ah monstrous
sweet monsters,
who spawned
thee chalk?
God? Who
Godded me?
Who me'd
God, chalk'd
Thought, &
Me sank
Down
To
Fall

A tché tché tcha
hoot ee
Wheet wha you—

Sweet monstranot love
By momma dears

Hey

Call God the Mother
To stop this fight

## 2ND CHORUS

Someday you'll be lying
there in a nice trance
and suddenly a hot
soapy brush will be
applied to your face
—it'll be unwelcome
—someday the
undertaker'll shave you

*

I almost called these poems
Pickpocket Blues
because they are the repetition
by memory
of earlier poems
stolen from me
b y  t w e l v e  t h i e v e s

## 3RD CHORUS

Ah monster sweet monster
Who spawned all this God
A Marva Ah Marvaila
Ah Marva Marvay
Ah marve  Ah Me
Ah John O Ah John
Oka John—
Where do you worka
John—Ah John,
How do you William the
Conqueror this morning
With your height old otay
—Nay, sight less worse,
Urp, the spur that did nape
At the wick the whack
Of the horse's piniard, urt,
So up heaved Pegasus
To rape the Sirens

And Black Bastards Hold Out their Arms

## 4TH CHORUS

One was called Boston Kitty—
He was a one-whack artist
Hold down the rope & the boy
And slip his villons i the store
—Oy—

This turp then, he was smart,
His wife was bloomer-hiding
Dress-thief, best, New York,
—Oir—

Ay
May the Wild Queen that Whanged
All the men with pipes
And ironingboard trays, i the
Movie bout paird?—
Waird!
Haird all about it in Dawson
Lass night, boys was tellin
The stove of the night
Hair—Robert Olson
Me that, Mrs Blake

## 5TH CHORUS

Pollyanna me that, Matt
Baker me Mary me Eddy
somethin bout life,—
Feed me T bone steaks
Off cows was allowed
Was allowed to be et
By men and maids
And Pomfranet

Poignardi me that,
hurt,—slip me the knife
in the chest, het—
they'll cut off my arms
and my losen legs
And my Peter Orlovsky
Clasel soul shall say:
Oido me no mo

## 6TH CHORUS

Ah moidnous two movies
Was railroad and et

Ah turpitude & turpentine
And serpentine & pine

Ah me star-veil
  that I see
Majesticking mightily
  on the rail
Of heaven-hailward
  high's moitang

Montana, me mountain,
Me Madonna, me high
Me most marvelous marvel
That held over the pie
Me sky of the Denver
Platte alley below

Me that me, me that me,
Me that me no more

## 7TH CHORUS

Brang!—blong!—trucks
Break glass i the dog barking
Street—dwang, wur,
Ta ta ta
  ta ta
Me that was weaned in the
  heaven's machine
Me that was wailed
  in the wild bar
called fence
Me that repeated & petered
The meter & lost 2 cents
Me that was fined
To be hined
And refined
    Ay
      Me that was
      Whoo ee
      The owl
      On the fence

## 8TH CHORUS

Me that was eyed
And betied by the eyes
In the glasses, In the Place,
In the night, brown beer,
Me that was maitled
And draitled and dragged
Me that was xarmined
By Murder Machree
Me that was blarnied
By Mary Carney
Me that was loved
Me that was hay
Me that the sunshine
Burned out every day
Me that was spotted
And beshatted
  By Marcus Magee

## 9TH CHORUS

Hey listen you poetry audiences
If you dont shut up
And listen to the potry,
See, we'll get a guy at the gate
To bar all potry haters
Forevermore

Then, if you dont like the subject
Of the poem that the poit
Is readin, geen, why dont
You try Marlon Brando
Who'll open your eyes
With his cry

James Dean is dead?—
Aint we all?
  Who aint dead—

John Barrymore is dead

Naw, San Francisco is dead
—San Francisco is bleat
  With the fog
(And the fences are cold)

## 10TH CHORUS

Old, San Francisco so old,
Shining garden on the end of the gate
Great plastic garden
Full of poets and hate

Fine wild bar place with high
Flootin dandies, Portugese,
Philippino, and just plain
Ole Dandy, Mandy tendin
The bar in the Brothers McCoy
On Sixth Street near Mission,
And Old Whitecap Sailor
Goes lonely the road
And Market Street on Sunday
There's no body broad
And O I see cliffside
With electrical magic
Message it me gives out
And sending Einstein
Me n McCorkle sit there
Eating in the Dharma

## 11TH CHORUS

We booted and we brained
Every seedy wet cold hill
And walked by rubber gardens
Behind telephones of shame
And came out mid the flowers
Of Heaven's O Gate

We treed every boner
Kited and committed
Longtailed and selffloored
And worked 78 to Del Monte
And back

Crashed Lux Perpetua
And tied up the mate
And dumped him down
In Chinatown
To Vegetate
So's cooks could clew garbage
And discover entrails
of babies made by Negresses
Against fences of taxis

## 12TH CHORUS

Soft!—the mysteries lie
In Eglantine

And Tathagata Nous Dit
Toujours, pas d secour,
    Pas d secour

Soft—pie-tailed bird-dog
Sing Song Charley the Poet
From High Masquerade
Is about to shake the rain
From his empty head
And deliver a blurbery statement
About bubbles and balloons

Balloons  O balloons
BALLOONS  BALLOONS
BALLOONS  O  BALLOONS
BAL
LOONS
B A L L O O N S

## 13TH CHORUS

When the rain falls on the Concord
And grapes are growing in New Hampshire
Mud hides wine bottles of green
And gay delight—When it rains
In Mexico, Oi Oi Oi, the swish
And plump and drenching Zapoteca
Big fat lump cacti growing in the night
Slipslop the sleeps of cats by the fence
And "Alms my youth!" cry women
To the passing Americano Oi—

Hate and oido, Old San Francisco's
Going to go—

Red, white and black, and blue
The pistil was tender when vines
Hund and daundered explosives
Of surrealistic pensioners

Dishrags have faces
Flashlights have hate
Pine trees are sweetest
To sit and meditate
The Holy Virgin of Heaven
Saw us in the rainy first morning

## 14TH CHORUS

Lost me Juju beads in the woods
And stood on dry stumps
    and looked around
And Lightning Creek morely roared
And wow the wild Jack Mountain
Abominable Snowman rooted
    in a stump
Even throwing football shadow
When games is ranging in the sky
Ah Gary,—would sweet Japan
Her gardens allay me
And make end sweet perfidy
—Full belly make you say
                nice things—
When rice bowl filled, Buddha frown
I' the West, because Wall of China
Has no holds

Holdfast to temple mountain chain
Throw away the halfdollars
Big and round, & wad of gum,
And flashlight lamp—& paint—
Go be shaved head monster
In a cave—No, tea ceremony
Beneath a sweet pine tree
        (Oi?)

## 15TH CHORUS

The little birds that live on the tree
In South America
Under clouds that make faces at me
Last night beautiful faces
Mad Dog McGoy of Heaven's
White Office, was sheening
His ocean spray at me
With holes for eyes
And every kind majesty—
Mocking at faces at me,
O me,—gingerale we drank
In Montreal when Errgang was young
And Wagner bleeded on the dump
And the dust of defeat perfidy
Was as fine as it is now
In the skies of untouchable dust
And Klings of the rooftop
Church variety—
My moity

## 16TH CHORUS

Auro Boralis Shomoheen
In the ancient blue Buick
Machine that cankers the highway
With Alice fat Queens, cards
Indexes burning, mapping machines,
Partings sweet sorrow
But O my patine

O my patinat pinkplat Mexican
  Canvas for oil in boil
Marrico—hash marsh m draw
The greenhouse bong eater from
fence N'awrleans, that—

Bat and be ready, Jesus is steady,
Score's eight to one, none,
Bone was the batter for McGoy
Poy—
        Used as this ditties
        for mopping the kitties
        in dream's afternoon
        when nap was a drape

## 17TH CHORUS

"Jamac! Jamac!
De bambi de bambi
Jamac jamac!"

And elegant old quorums
of fortified priests
sighed

De bambi de bambi jamac
Jamac, and eldertwine
old tweedies fighted the prize

"Parrac! Motak!
Pastamak arrac!
Arrash!
Crrash!"

Part art tee
tea symphony
ceremonious old bonious
me love you
me

## 18TH CHORUS

Henry Regalado, l'hero de la
Bataille de Patenaud

God and all the other little people

Esmack, esmack, I esmacka
You on the kisser you too
I thrun nobody oud dis joint
Since Roosevelt had all his joints

And Buddy I knowed
That old Patenaude
Was a fraude from the start,
Tonio me Kruger you that,
Hat—
Pat was the rat that had the hat

Mash patinaud
Crash toutes les shows
Grange toutes les villes
  les jilles
Mange toutes les filles

## 19TH CHORUS

The diamond that cuts through
To the other view
That I painted all white for you
I edited your rough stone,
Produced a diamond show,
Elephantine was the mine
Eglantine adamant and mad
  And madly adamantine
  My Allah you mine,
  The diamond of Dipankar
  The prime ripe wreak havoc
  Buddha pra-teeth torn
  Mouth Ya-Hoi-Ya-Hai
  Pastumintapaling porpitoi
  Turnpot of biled pata taters
  Smater Gater the Mater
  O'Shay, rife was the weather
  Was singin was gay,
  Rape were the weathers
  In heaven's O Shay

## 20TH CHORUS

Old buddy aint you gonna stay by me?
Didnt we say I'd die by a lonesome tree
And you come and dont cut me down
But I'm lying as I be
Under a deathsome tree
Under a headache cross
Under a powerful boss
Under a hoss
(my kingdom for a hoss
a hoss
fork a hoss and head
for ole Mexico)
Joe, aint you my buddy thee?
And stay by me, when I fall & die
In the apricot field
And you, blue moon, what you doon
Shining in the sky
With a glass of port wine
In your eye
—Ladies, let fall your drapes
and we'll have an evening
of interesting rapes
inneresting rapes

## 21ST CHORUS

Let fall the interesting fall
And I lie and be as I be

He stayed up in my case
for quite awhile

Tremendous pace—He was
A petty thief or he'd sell junk
One or the other

I did my best to keep him from
selling junk

French fag from Montreal
Hid the capsules up his ass
And took em out in a restaurant
On Broadway and Ninety Sixth

And I went to Eighty Sixth
Those girls hit up on me
"Man is here!"
And I bought four more caps

And the fag went home with a girl
What a beautiful shape
that woman had

## 22ND CHORUS

Ha well dear and Ah Men
The wee girl that was comin again
She was for the books
 The Ursula plea
 That I could not take

O you better baike
  O you better bake
  A better cake than this
O you better Miss
Yes you better miss
When the thing never will kwiss

O sweetheart and okay
Here's hopin we'll all be away
  It was great fun
But it was just one a
    those tings

## 23RD CHORUS

Dom dum dom domry
Dom—dom—hahem—
Sum—(creeeeee!)—Hnf—
Shh—Hnf—Shh—Haf
Shhh—Shhh—Hiffff—
—Ma—
Snffff—(bing bring, se ting)
—"Yo conee na nache"—
D ding—d ding—d-ding—
Cramp!—O ya ta dee
—ker blum—kheum—
Hnffff—drrrrrrrr—drosh—
Pepock—Shiffle—t bda—
Want a piece a bread
No
Jack? Hnff—Ta ra ta ra fuee
—Te wa ta ra teur—
Grrr—he na pa powa shetaw—
Tck tick tick Today is Sunday

## 24TH CHORUS

Eternally the lightning runs
Through form after form formless
In positive and negative repose

It makes no difference that your uncle
Was black with sufferance & bile,
The whild childscriming skies will
Always be the muchacho same

Much words been written about it
The message from infinite
That will be was brought to us
Is one
But because it has no name
We can only call it Bibit
    "It was Liebernaut who had
      the dream of uncovering Carthage"
The snow in the sea mountains

## 25TH CHORUS

In Egypt under rosebushes
Fifi's fruits & sweets

My Egyptian connection's
Gonna be late, the conductor
Wouldnt take my change

The Egyptian conductor
Wouldnt nod

Sandalwood and piss and pulque
Burning in every door,
Mighty Marabuda River
Flows along

Sampans and river thieves
And woodsplitters and blind
Thieves' Markets & imbeciles
"See Milan and see the world"

Heppatity the twat kid
Hatted by the racetrack
Horses' moon barns
spun on a gibbee
For lying alone

## 26TH CHORUS

My poems were stolen
    by Fellaheen Thieves
In the city of the midnight

The title was "Fellaheen Blues"
And justice is done to Rome

I'll never see them again
Learn what sweet development
I'd harbored up to meditate
All's left now
        is these hateful
        New Fallaheen Blues
        which mean nothing
        and I hate them
In the other book I cried
Ah-da  Ah-da
  the parturient spinsters
  that prate i the dining hill
  Are having blue venison
  To goose their old hyms
    Og

## 27TH CHORUS

But I'll tell you—electricity
Runs through all these forms
And we call it electricity
And notice the forms
But what's hoppen in nothin
Is wha hoppen in nothin
    See?
    The butchers a de Bronx
    Ourter now dat

—the late night tweed diners
Italian restaurants on Bleecker
that sing in the staring blue street
with cigarettes of legs
  Ourter know dat
The wild outflow wow open
O gate of golden honey
Hopin hill up above
And below & within
The kin, aye, my,
What a roseate balloon
For lovers of kin

## 28TH CHORUS

Part of the morning stars
  The moon and the mail
The ravenous X, the raving ache,
—the moon Sittle La
Pottle, teh, teh, teh,—
The tatata of thusness
Twatting everywhere—

  The poets in owlish old rooms
  who write bent over words
  know that words were invented
  Because nothing was nothing

In use of words, use words,
the X and the blank
And the Emperor's white page
And the last of the Bulls
Before spring operates
Are all lotsa nothin
  which we got anyway
So we'll deal in the night
  in the market of words

## 29TH CHORUS

And he sits embrowned
  in a brown chest
Before the palish priests

And he points delicately
  at the sky
With palm and forefinger

And's got a halo
  of gate black

And's got a hawknosed
  watcher who loves to hate

But has learned to meditate
  It do no good to hate

So watches, roseate laurel
  on head
In back of Prince Avolokitesvar
  Who moos with snow hand
And laces with pearls
  the sea's majesty

## 30TH CHORUS

The little bug thrasheth
on the table
Hungry to burn in the candle
of flames
Jerks at the gate-bottoms
of wax cold hide
Albions and Albans
to his little sight
Leaps to be browned
in the roast rite
Soars & tries to reach
dizzy height
Falls in the temples
and quivers & slaps
Playin like a schoolboy
in the valleys
Of silver & ivory hate

## 31ST CHORUS

I

I had a slouch hat too one time
The old slouch hat
I just keep walkin around
And he keeps walkin around with me
Around and round that necktie
  counter we went
When it rained I wore my old
    slouch hat

It was a good felt that
  I had to carry through many
  rainy day, late fall
  and the early spring

Perhaps it was a rainy day
And the house dick mighta saw
My hat
      Each tie on that ring
      Worth six bucks, Brooks Brothers,
      Sixty bucks wortha ties
Slacks with peculiarities
I couldnt even find a pair of slacks
I thought it was suitable to wear

## 32ND CHORUS

II

Wrapped one pair around me
And pinned it with a safety pin
And pulled up my trousers and
  Went out looked at myself in the mirror
    'O no, those wont do'
    And I walked out

Wrap the slacks around my waist

Took two other pair
    went to the mirror
  threw them at the salesman
'No those wont do—good
    afternoon' and walked out

The slouch hat I got at Harvard
    Club, Yale Club, Princeton Club
    one or the other
    Dartmouth Club
    University Club

Always barred the Yatch Club
    because it was a little over
    my kin

## 33RD CHORUS

III

The doorman knew that only
Mr Astor Mr Vanderbilt
Mr Whitney belonged

He couldnt say 'Good morning
Mister Astor' because
he knew I wasnt Mister
Astor

I always figured a way to heel
into those other clubs

Not only a member of Who's
Who but a Who's Who
also have to be a member
of Who's Who in New York
in the special clique of Who's

Hoo—slouch hat!

I get in the Athletic Club
many time

## 34TH CHORUS

IV

And I'd go up in the Billiard Room
And I would wander back around
The room, hands in back,
And every coat rack I backed
Up against feel for the wallet
One day I walked
Outa there with ten wallets

Bellboy lookin me over
Pretty soon a very dignified looking
gentleman came up and buzzed
the bell boy

He says "Who?" and I says
"Man told me his name, while
We're drinkin at the bar,
And told me to meet him
In the billiard-room
of the Athletic Club
I dont see him—so I best I
better go"

## 35TH CHORUS

V

"Tell me about the old slouch
hat"

One of my numerous trips
to one of the numerous clubs
in New York City

The hat finally was left
in the hotel
which I had to leave
rather hurriedly one night
never to return
so the hat was given
to the castoffs of the hotel
which they collect
and rummage sells

May now be worn by one
Of the members of Skid Row

New York City—the Bowery

"I seen that hat
by moonlight"

## 36TH CHORUS

VI

I had a pointed mustache
and I mean pointed
half inch from here

Double breasted vest
and a Derby hat
and striped trousers
English shoes, black,
very pointed, they were
Hannah Shoes

People on Broadway'd turn
and look at me

The worst is yet to come
I had a pince nez
with a long black ribbon
to my buttonhole

And I wore a carnation
white or red

Boy did I look like somethin

## 37TH CHORUS

### VII

A year later I got caught
I was dressed differently
    and everything
But boy that mustache
    and that pince nez
    was really out of this world

I used that outfit six months
I finally had to pack it in
  because it was too well-worn

Pince nez was in a coat
  I stole
Mustache I grew in the
    sanitarium
While taking one of my
    numerous drug cures

My mother'd come to see me
    She says "Oh No!
    Cut it off!"
"I'm just havin a little fun, mother"

## 38TH CHORUS

### VIII

Took it on the lam
And went to Canada

late at night I'm fulla
  morphine and I come down
  fulla goofballs too

This guy had ventriloquist doll
And he gave out this Texas Guinan
Routine "Hello Sucker, we
like your money as well
as anybody else's—s matter
of fact the bigger your roll
the more we take ya"

He used to get everybody
  interested with the doll
  and cutout silhouettes
  put stripes in your tie

Wound up in his room
  gave him a shot of morphine

## 39TH CHORUS

### IX

Out on the highway I thumbed a ride
into Buffalo and I put the bum
on the guy for something to eat
—'Eat in my drugstore'—
So we went in the back
And he had corn on the cob
And boiled potatos, 'Say fellow
I always hear people talk
about morphine, what's it look
like?'—he shows me—he
had a key a cabinet and
he had bottles of hundreds
quartergrains halfgrains
pantapon delauddit everything
and soon as he tended
the customers I emptied the
bottles—got outa there pretty
quick, bought a safety pin
in Buffalo and took a shot
in the toilet

## 40TH CHORUS

X

Come out and saw a fellow
shaving, his coat hanging there,
hung my own coat and gave
his coat a brush of my hand,
felt his wallet, washed my hands,
and went out and took off
with the wallet

So I started out on a shoplifting
campaign in Buffalo
    wasnt very experienced at it

Started out with a topcoat
and I sold it in a taxicab stand

Next day I decided to get myself
some suits
        and I went up
        I had a suitbox
I walked about & put the suitbox
in one of the dressingrooms
    Looked & fooled in the mirror
    Went out, I hocked those two

## 41ST CHORUS

### XI

Next day like a damn fool
go out to the same store
but I got a newspaper
instead of a suitbox
    thought I'd try
    a new routine

Two guys kinda watchin me
I went in wrapped myself up
two suits
        went in the elevator
        bottom gentleman
        tapped me on the arm
        'Will you come with me
                please?'

And the County Jail they ate
breakfast and got oatmeal
with one spoonful of molasses,
for lunch stew, mostly bones,
Graveyard Stew, and for supper
    dinner at night
Beans—and you couldnt smoke

►•◄

## 42ND CHORUS

Kayo Mullins is always yelling
and stealing old men's shoes
Moon comes home drunk, kerplunk,
Somebody hit him with a pisspot
Major Hoople's always harrumfing
Egad kaff kaff all that
Showing little kids fly kites right
And breaking windows of fame

Blemish me Lil Abner is gone
His brother is okay, Daisy Mae
and the Wolf-Gal

Ah who cares?
Subjects make me sick
all I want is C'est Foi
Hope one time
bullshit in the tree

Hmmmmmmmmmmmmmmm
I've had enough of foolin me
And making silly imagery
Harrumph me katt
I think I'll take off
For Cat and fish

## 43RD CHORUS

Well & well well, so that's
The ancient fainter, the painter
Who tied up blue balloons
—Globas azul—and threw
Them asunder in the thunder
Of the ul—Ur—Obi—Ob-
Fuscate me no more travails,
Pardy hard, this rock mine
We're workin'll yield up diamond
hard

And then we'll cut thru conceptions
And come with answer pard

And what twill it be, sorry pard,
Aint never no mystery
Was imparted to me
Lessn you wanta try Roy McGoon
Who learned it in Innisfree

Or old Yow O Yeats, Blake,

We havent got the diamond tho
That freed Dipankara Buddha
In the Palaeolithic morning
And made him make faces
In Samapattis at me
Let's free

## 44TH CHORUS

High Cascades or Mexico—
headaches
Travel everywhere

Forms and costumes and noses
All this changing literature
Cyrano de Bergerac, King
of the French underworld
King for a day, Henry V,
Falstaff his father, Henry IV,
Warlike stools frowning in
'We have no more use
For your caisson iron,
It's too fat
and the water too vile,
I'll vouch for the master
but water your while
had better be bile
to judge from the green
of the innocent liquid'
Reading, naught, words, styles
The only thing matter is otay

## 45TH CHORUS

English Literature
    a School of Writing

French Literature
    was closed off

How tight the lips of Zola the
                Master

Wont tell how he grips his pen
To consorts of learners

English, Old Shakespeare gathered
    bout him minor figures
    like Ben Jonson
    Maurie O'Tay
    Henry Fenelon
    And Molly O'Day

Irish Literature—that was
  where the brabac originated
  from
    Wood cracking in the sea

## 46TH CHORUS

And what is God?
The unspeakable, the untellable,
—
Rejoice in the Lamb, sang
  Christopher Smart, who
  drives me crazy, because
  he's so smart, and I'm
  so smart, and both of us
  are crazy

No,—what is God?
The impossible, the impeachable
Unimpeachable Prezi-dent
of the Pepsodent Universe
but with no body & no brain
no business and no tie
no candle and no high
no wise and no smart guy
no nothing, no no nothing,
no anything, no-word, yes-word,
everything, anything, God,
the guy that aint a guy,
the thing that cant be
and can
and is
and isnt

## 47TH CHORUS

Beverly Dickinson, wasnt it,
the distraught perfect poetess
who lived in New Hampshire
and wrote about roots & roses

Sweet old Beverly I remember her well
and her attic was fragrant,
her Attican divine
her storm bird
her fence story
her bee inside
her butterfly
her broom
her Majesty
the Queen

Said, "Emily Dickinson is as great
as Shakespeare sometimes,"
said T. S. Eliot's editor
Robert Giroux, swell fellow—
Her Attic divine, her antic,
—her

Sang in the blue hill
    her larks and mimes
And died all a silent
    in her prophecy tomb

## 48TH CHORUS

Dans son tombeau
Elle a gagnée
Toutes les lignes noires
D'Eternité

Que' s' trouve dans la terre
Quand qu'l mouille dans l'Hiver

Salonge!—Mompress!
Traboune!—Partance!

Elle a trouvée dejas
L'ange d'Archanciel
Couchez dans la mer
D'été d'nuée

Aye, oui, mes Anges toutes Francais
Mes tours d'ircanciel

Ma miel, mon or,
Mes ames deshonorées,
Mes troublages, mes lignes,
Mon vin sur la table
Ou sur le plancher

## 49TH CHORUS

Book of Dreams
(Written in dream language)
Old Hosapho we wont let up
And hear me sing the
hm—Ole Hosapho
he wont let me record
me dream language

Ooogh! he upped & come back
Ole Hosapho
But now he's down's
Gone down boy again

Hay Hosapho, say sumptin!
Hoy Hosapho, Roil!
Nope Hosapho stay lead down
—A mani a Gloria—
Tinkle tinkle laughter
Dingle little pretties
everything's happening everywhere

## 50TH CHORUS

My real choice was to go
to Princeton—I wanted
to be orange and black
on the football field

and orange Varsity letters
on black wool jackets
with buttons, and elm trees
and Sunday afternoon
the swish of the snow
and Einstein in his yard
and All's Well with
the Emily Dickinson world

And drive to New Hope
    for a drink
    or lobster

And take the sad train
on the platform of night
And ride into riot New York
On a Saturday Night
To go see Count Basie
Baying at the Lincoln
With Lester Otay Young
On Tenor Saxophone

## 51ST CHORUS

Boy, sa den du coeur, sa, le bon
vin—Mama, c'est'l'port
si fort, le vin divin—

Aye, oui, mais écoute—dans
les milieus de les nuits,
tu wé, sa den du coeur,
sa den du coeur

Ca fa du bien au beson

Besoigne?—Di mué pas la
besogne maudit, la bédenne,
maudit, la bédenne,
  sa fa du bien a bédenne
    pauvr' bédenne

A, y parle tu aussi bien
    q'ca
      a Milan
    les Italiens a gueules
Nous autres aussi on a une
belle lagne qui clacke

## 52ND CHORUS

Dog with mouths, in Navajoa,
bent down to the mud
and slippered shining entrails
in the morning Sinaloa sun
of a dead rabbit

Then the bus come and run
  it over, the rabbit, sullen
  dog skimpered off a minute,
  came back to repeat his
        refection

Oh well, shiney priests
      eat goodies
      in every store they see

Old Navajoa shit dog, you,
your goodies are the goodiest
goodies I ever did see, how
dog you shore look mad
when yer bayin

Hoo Hound-dog!
    dont eat that dead rabbit
    in front of my face raw
    —cook it a lil bit

## 53RD CHORUS

I had a scrap with a doctor
one night
We were both drunk
I said "Just because you're
a doctor you think you're
so smart, if you're
going to report me go
ahead you prick"

And I fell off the stool
I was fulla goofballs

He went to the other doctor
"You better look this guy
up, he must be some kind
of a phoney"

Pony the pony the pony
the pra
Pony the pony the pony
the pra

## 54TH CHORUS

I got a grass jaw, boys,
I say, and knock out Ray
Robinson in the first minute
of the first round

Then they bring in Tiger Jones
because I made no bones
about how I was out to
Kayo Robinson, moonbless him

Tiger Jones comes on me all
fists, hard puncher, I got
nothing to do but retreat
or turn into grass, so
 I dance
 right in
 to his arms
   reach
and plow him all over
with crazy little punches
some of which are hard
    and we wake up

## 55TH CHORUS

Someday they'll have monuments
set up to reverend the mad
people of today in madhouses

As early pioneers in the knowing
that when you lose your reason
you attain highest perfect knowing

Which is devoid of predicates
such as: "I am, I will, I reason—"
—devoid of saying:-"I will do it"
—devoid

Devoid of insanity as well by virtue
    of no contact

But meanwhile these deterministic
doctors really do believe that mad
is mad—

And have erected a billion-dollar
religion to it, called, Psycho-medicine,
and ah—

Well we'll know the sanity
    of Ard Bar

In the morning, some time, alone

## 56TH CHORUS

Some'll go mad with numbers
Some'll go mad with words

Some'll pretend to lose reason
And lose reason anyway

Some wont, some'll be secret,
Some'll screw in long black
rooms
With the fantastic short-haired
Beauty who lies on the bed
listening

To Sinatra—some'll be candleflame
jiggling gently in the night

Some'll be racetrack operators,
some'll have soap in their pockets

Some'll sing in the Bronx Jail
and some wont sing in Riker's

Some'll come out of it
with iron heads

Some'll wear coats
and hard of it

## 57TH CHORUS

The monstrous jailer, he wouldnt let me
  outa that jailhouse—
    till I had smoked all the tea
    I could smoke, 'Finish up!'
    he said, & prodded me

And I gotta take big long hikes
  of draw on that cigarette tree

How'd I get outa that jail?
  By forgetting all about me

Which was the best rasperry tree
They ever ternevented in ole
Donnesfree
Cause I figure there's no difference
twixt me and dead dog mud
Made of bones and take your pick,
    sulphur or Innisfree

How'd they ever get that tap
    outa me?
Wasnt I tired givin?
    hard tap
Family tree.
I wasnt sweet givin.

## 58TH CHORUS

Las ombras vengadora
they say in little taco joints
when the shadows are coming
at about dusk-time, in Azteca,
modern Fellaheena Mexico,
Las ombras vengadora
Lass ombras venga dora
Most beautiful sound in the world
    hep!
  Swing up the team, bring up
    the gangs, say, didnt I yell
    at you a minute ago?

Hoy!
    Las ombras vengadora
    in little taco sad joints
    on Sunday Afternoon
    and fathers are home
    honoring their sons

## 59TH CHORUS

Fantasm crazam crazam
Joe Kennedy stops me on
  the sidewalk of the Immemorial
University—ack hook
You got your prick out.

I look down, no such thing

What are your two balls
doing hanging on the sidewalk?

I think I'll squat & shit—
We both squat facing each
  other on the campus
If ya know what I mean,
  cream, we squat
practice 'mitate Aristophanes
and sit there too laughing
and talking, Kennedy,
one of my first mature
  Irishmen

Face each other with feet
partly out, like in Esquire
the phonies showing their shoes
  Squat n Shit!

## 60TH CHORUS

I purified language early in my
young days, I purified & squatted
& beshitted on pages, sophomore,
on my typewriter, all the dirty
words I could think of
        squrify & squat & shit
And slit—and finally I'm
in history class & the professor
says 'Kerouac—what you
dreamin about?'
And I shhoudda said Ack—
Pack—Squrify and squat
and shit, who wants to hear
about the aniards and breast
plates of warriors of the
        Medieval Ages
I wanta know about the people
on the street, what they doin?
And what the high art
hark squambling in his quiet
  temple moonlit gambymoon
writing jingles & jongles
      for the pretties on the square

## 61ST CHORUS

Orizaba Rooftop blues
Listenin to the street news
Saturday night down there
Pleep! went the new little bike
    horn
As the cat pleeped it with his
Foot zinging the bike across
the fantastic bus-driven corners
Barging everywhere, he just angles
    and amples
    like Stan Getz on tenor
And swings around right around
    the fender okay

Orizaba rooftop, Orizaba Rooftop,
Blue, blue, blue
Blue's made of shiny everyway

Orizaba honk-honk, bus motors
Riding high for the clutch, tired,
Faces green on the benches,
Ikons in the corner
        Tails of little fenelet
        serpents hanging from the fender

Aik, motorcycle of no-cops,
Hotrods & Deans of Mexico,
Aik, aik, aik Mexico
        BORRACHO GUAPO BANJO

## 62ND CHORUS

Pipestoon the Ribber & wobbed
old ladies of shame. the same.
party twan twit Twittenden
Charley, 'Awfully good fuck!'
  he yells out the train window,
  to his waving host of the weekend,
'I say old chap, really!!'
and then Commando Poltroon
  comes platooning up in mudsplash,
  Monty, examining every commando
  standing naked in the rain,
    'That hurt?' whacking
    a guy on the rib, 'No
  sir,' 'Why not?'
      'Commando, sir'
Finally he comes to a man
with a long hardon, & whacks
it with his military crop
—with his baton—
'That hurt?'  'No sir'
            "Why not?"
  "Man behind me sir."

## 63RD CHORUS

The star is reflected in the puddle
and the star dont care
and the puddle dont care
Nothing is thinking
not even the puddle poet

That's why "This Thinking Has Stopped"
Is the best way I know to imitate
this starry state of affairs
in puddles

Plass! plash!—wait a minute!—
wait a second buddy while I
hock up old Desroches three
sacrifices

For each sacrifice you're reborn
and you're only reborn once
because there is only One
Sin

Slatter me pet Charley, T-rod,
pettle pole and all, believes,
and goes rosing in the woods

Purt! Foley! Words! Names!
Ahab, Starbuck & Pip
Iago and Poltroon
and Pipestaff the Ribber
—pain, pain, the no-name retoin

## 64TH CHORUS

On the street I seen three guys
standing talking quietly in the sun
and suddenly one guy leaps in pain
and whacks his fingers in the air
as he's burned his hand
    with a match
    lighting a butt

The other two guys dont even
    know this,
they go right on talking
    gesticulating with hands

I seen it, it was on San Jose
    Boulevard in St Joseph
    Missouri, nineteen thirty
    two

Them guys didnt even realize
pain is one thing, everywhere?

    Whai? Every golden
    sweetgirl come & befawdle
    her pillow in my hair
        and I dont care?
            Wha?

## 65TH CHORUS

### JEWISH GOY IN N.Y.

Wha? Whaddayou mean,
there are ten thousands mysteries
of me by the millions standing
with hand-molded shows
and sports jacket
and no hair

bouncing along in one long corridor
of images in a mirror
into infinity
eternity
call it what you will!

I know that!—You dont have
pull that Buddha-stuff
on me, Jack, I dont care

I've seen me in the picture
stretched out everywhere
it dont matter?
Who cares!

I go to Lefty's & eat pastrami
on Sunday afternoon,
with mustard—I go hear
some music at Carnegie Hall
—I lay my wife—
I sit on the bed, work

Who cares? Wha?
What's the moon got?

## 66TH CHORUS

What's the moon got but tunes?
Wha? I dont care I'll talk
I'll stand right here talk
till doomsday, nobody care,
nobody say, who knows? who
wants? What's gonna free
what from what? Shit!
  Gold! Girl! Honey! Call!
  What you will, call it,
  shit, I'll sit, I'll talk,
  I'll hang all day, because,
  it doesnt matter, you talk
  about it doesnt matter
  but you dont realize how
  doesnt-matter
  it really doesnt-matters,

        Wow man, I mean,

Sure, shoes, Shows, Hand
painted molds from azimuth
shoes, azipeth azipor
azinine blues, you got,
who cares, tsawright, eat,
pickles in the barrel—
  ——hail a cab—
      do what you want

## 67TH CHORUS

"It all goes down the same hole"
said Allen, eating cake & food
in a restaurant, with milk
in his coffee, no milk in the can,
no sense in the sour bottom
of that can

All goes up the same sky,
  all sucks on same air,
all plops drops impregnates
  and saves anywhere
The same limitation gentiles
    the crave for a show
on notwithstanding lost bibles
    dedicating the mystery
to a vain empty show,
'Vanity of Vanities,
      All is Vanity'
"Behold her breasts are like
    fawns"
    in the summer air,
Her eyes are like doves,
    skin like the tents
—Skin like the rents
in the heavenly air

## 68TH CHORUS

A murder  stern gird
A million dollar ba by
Ack
  Rowers of galleys,
  Candle lights,
  Hearners of yorn,
  Parturient ones,
  Poo,
  Patch art part tea
  Gart and band thee
  Harden thy garkle
  And get ye no purple kirtles
  Ere aye mice Burns
  Hands Mc Caedmon let loose
  His last tired crazy pom
        'Hung la terre,
        hang the twarrie,
      part de twaklockleme,
    gockle somackle magee'

    Down with the back rooms
    Of Dublin

## 69TH CHORUS

### PRAYER

God, protect me!
  See that I dont defecate
    on the Holy See

See that I dont
  murder the bee

God! be kind!
  Free all your dedicate
    angels, for me

Or if not for me
    for anybody

God!  Hold fast!
  I'm dying in your arms
    delicately

Ah God be merciful
    to Princeton me

Ah God, alack a God,
  nobody farms
    amnesty

## 70TH CHORUS

I

There'll be no more ginger ale
for me
goodbye ginger ale
when I die
in Innisfree

That's where I'll go to die
to look and die
I'll never go there now

Because I've already told the boys
at the paper
the sound is crashing me

And they ate paper
And it was a paper party

But when the bell bonged toll,
And we all had to pay,
"Die in my arms, lamb,"
sang Rudy Vallee
from here to eternity

Die in my that's a beautiful arms,
    lad,
Die in my that's a beautiful arms,
    said God
To me

## 71ST CHORUS

II

That's just something
that isnt written
in Wells' history

That's something, Window Knock,
when you can make me
pray me

That'll do the reading
in London Library

And in Dublin I is free
To read
Old Innisfree

And then I'll read Finn
Again, and meet Magee
In a back alley

And get to know
    Donnelly
And the brothers Donnelly

That's where I'll be,
    My Arma Carney,
I'll be dyin
  down in Innisfree
Waiting for ye
Mary Carney

# ORLANDA BLUES

## 1ST CHORUS

Le corp de la verité
pourre dans la terre

The body of truth
rots in the earth

nourriture dans la terre

Sanchez fourwinds bigtown,
dont wail that at me
  Fraserville Quebec
    comes back to me

  In the night sun sleep
  warm, store it in tanks

Blues of Old Virginia tree
      moonbottles over kiss time
    listener appeal
      Kissland
          Kissimee Florida
These are Orlanda Blues

## 2ND CHORUS

O Cross on my wall
  O body of Christ

When I was awright
  Saturday night

Little in your arms
  your thousands of years

In electric resist I wanted
  to soul the liking I saw
—*words*

(musician pauses)

## 3RD CHORUS

This book is too nice for me
They made Clay Felker editor
of Esquire
Or Rust Hills one
and what ever happened to glass
and the joke about the Lord.

The Lord is my Agent.

My message is blah blah blah

My yort tackalitwingingly
  pasta vala tt, yea, p,
  my reurnent gollagigle
  dil plat most-rat, my
    erneealieing cralmaa
    tooth, ant, mop, sh,
  my devoid less 2 immensity
  secret muzning midnight,
  my whatzit
        you wanta
            know
                Whatzit!
      Joy  Look out!

## 4TH CHORUS

Joy look in,
look in,
the pretty
sin

Loy, t a tt ct b
I fooled with the long
overload
(wrong over road?)
wronk

What a moistious wronk
we're in fair words,
or is it wairds
in your part
of the
Kelp,
Laird

In Scotland we just throw
the bones to the dogs
& toast at the
fireplace

## 5TH CHORUS

Well then let's have a toast
I wonder if I can write
poems just like Gregory
Croso:—let's see:—
The dead are dead,
I'll resurrect them with
this song, O fall
you fair held
cities—
(wood wood wood)
O held the fair held
in the skinny bar!
(the skinny bar held Indian
sonofabitch)
So North Mood wrote:—
C o l t i n g—The Gregory
says "Eels & gripplings
in
my
eaves"

## 6TH CHORUS

Finally I was in Stockholm at last
Cold night
  Dark in Swedenborg

Zeldipeldi my junkey friend
  from N.Y. and Maldo
  Saldo the hot trumpeter
    from Nigeria, turned on
    in the cold room overlooking
      black rooftops of winter,
        Sweden night skies February,
          Ommani pahdme hom

I wanted to catch a train
      to the Capital

I was on a seacoast town,
 the name of it was Fidel
 or Fido
        wow, mominu,
        You dont know how far
              that sky
                go

## 7TH CHORUS

Message from Orlanda:—
You guys cant explore
all of outer space, unless
you want to spend
a million million million
million million million
billion billion bullion
bullion years at it
—and when you gets
there, and you cant
even get there, give my
regards to Captain Bligh

And lissen, before you leave,
how bringin my money
with you to preserve
in eternity, see, I
can cash in when
I get there & spend it
on
space
travel

## 8TH CHORUS

Thats awright, space'll carry
us maybe like little eggs,
the buggy children work
their way out
to the surface
of the egg,
to the shell,
they swim soft,
& they get there
& meet God
The Shell
The Shell
hard & cold
against the cold
gray sun
blood
in
your
Father's
Long Winter
Underwear

So sleep

## 9TH CHORUS

Me, I'm worried I'm a secret sinner
and God
Ole Tangerine
I call Him
because one day I was settin
under trees
in
a
chair

And deciding what name
to give to God, is it
a personal God? & blam
the little tangerine
landed
squarely
on my
head
like Newton's
underwear,

& so I saw it personal
And I say the moral is simple

## 10TH CHORUS

But it landed right on the
tippy tiptop
of the sconce,
Jazz,
dazz,
and that's why I believe
(since it's all grinning
in there)
it was a little
tap reminder

I dont *need* thunderclouds!

"Maybe Eden aint so
lonesome as New England
used to be," said Emily
Dickinson sitting with
a tangerine in her hand

(They shipped it from Cuba)
It was a great show
Gasser!

## 11TH CHORUS

I guess God is alright
He'll take care of us

But there are perturbing roots
in these trees,
that claw in earth
& outa fingernails
as long as Malaya
eat up thru sucktubes
the juice of the mother
Terra Firma
Mona Leisure

& these roots remind you
of the roots in your grave
I wish I could be cremated
& sprung
(to the wave),
but Ah, hell, I donno
I think I'll go to
Sapplewhile
& idle away the
unfinished poem

## 12TH CHORUS

The evening silencius
Poetry
    is so pretty
 When you silence it like that

It's nice to pop pearl pages
the candlelight, you know,
    is dedicated to poets

Okay—dreaming fields—Blake
wants to hear the latest development
in the man the way the bleat
lambs bleakly blake it now
and that is soft,
        Ah William,
    I guess as soft as Spanish
    dreams, what was it Trappist
     said:— "Goats
                as
                soft
                as
                sleep"
 Something like that
      Farewell

## 13TH CHORUS

Jack Micheline
"Feet of children playing by
the mill"—he didnt say
hill—When tongue gets
caught inside the lapels
of the mouth, that's what
I wanta hear—Like Fred
Katz the cellist—or is
it chellist?

"Tongue crucified, seven stitched"
is pretty weird

Make it down to New Orleans
one of these days
says Moonlight Martin

"Maniac massacred" on account
of "blinded on stone"
Wow, whatze mean?
Like Wolfe's Underground, mad dog
choking in tunnels of hate
"Spring has come
yellow teeth & black hair"

## 14TH CHORUS

is exactly like the magnificent
haiku mailed to President
Eisenhower by Manosuke
Kambe
"They have succeeded
in shooting up a star
And Spring is near"

Yeah, where down yonder
in you now Where

Now I'm getting to sound
like a drearisome
tangerine

Folks, read Jack Micheline,
n doubt about it
He's a great poeit
And see?—read Gregory Corso
too all about "bookies
& chickenpluckers"
& Read Competition Ginsberg
the maddest brain
in poetry

## 15TH CHORUS

Ginsberg has a poet who
has a "great precise
practical benevolence
& new understanding,"
and I have Jack
Micheline, Steve Tropp,
Steve White, and
many other naked heads
What I wrote first I kept,
because I figure
God moves
the body hand
because
the body of the truth
is a body
corruptible
in graves
though
nourishing,
O Schweitzer
Africa Trumpet!

## 16TH CHORUS

(And George Jones blows too!)

"Kneeling in the sun beside
the bright red mad beauties
of Street!" sings Corso

"I drag him into
myricolorous St Chapelle
Stained Glass marvel,"
sings Ginsberg

Dont discourage
the poets!

Sings Jack Micheline:
"And kiss the strangers
& plant the seeds of life among the dead"

Because it's a distant
hightone rail
"Flower of cities"

## 17TH CHORUS

And these sweet lines revive
the open poetry of hope
in old America
long fish

And this sweet moth revised
the entelechy
in my endebechy
in old pardodechy
where Croo-Ba
made it working
boy girls in

He was hanged in the closet
The King ate sliced sage
John the Baptist had no head
Jesus had nails in his skin
The Neon's nailed to me
I wish I were dead
Or King of Ronald Colman
country, or Kin to Sariputra
Shakespeare, one

## 18TH CHORUS

Well, s'long as barrel womps we'll
  womp em on in, Used to write
  poems about Princeton boy rose

Also Baltimore bleedings
  & think rabbit plate
shit
 I wish I had
    a way
      to make
        Tuesday Sarah
          come by
            any day

With China throwup
    hadnt Puttered
    men with me

  but bile was free,
      & girl long blonde
        taffy pull

I guess best thing to do
  is to write to
  Blues Bessie

## 19TH CHORUS

I wonder what Emily's thinkin
in that groomus earth of
coral snakes & alligators
on the sidewalk, is she got down
by Sunday in the Tomb, or
does time matter no blow out
bulbs of shame, Jesus, what
shame in eyelid war life
no shame at all in eyelid
ant eat

allied ant eat
What wars Bismarck plotted
on accounta ambitious
bishops, I dont know,
what Colbert built
for Mazarin slurp,
or why French Blond
Hero bombs black
Arab dream in sand
of Berber Ya ke
Silhouette Blue men
veil, kill me, I'se
free

## 20TH CHORUS

Jazz killed itself
But dont let poetry kill itself
Dont be afraid
of the cold night air

Dont listen to institutions
When you return manuscripts to
brownstone
dont bow & scuffle
for Edith Wharton pioneers
or ursula major nebraska prose
just hang in your own backyard
& laugh play pretty
cake trombone
& if somebody gives you beads
juju, jew, or otherwise,
sleep with em around your neck
Your dreams'll maybe better

There's no rain,
there's no me,
I'm telling ya man
sure as shit

## 21ST CHORUS

That cat's in paradise
The noise of automobile sigh
dont interfere with the knowing
of me or any paper party
but's what smat smeldied
on hey-now, Zulch!

Truth is, cry

Because the radar never was invented
could find paradise sound
or cat lost in the night
radarless
radar-less
rad-arless
radarle-ss

rrrrt
branged suitcases as a kid
& sang to Glenn Miller's
Moonlight Serenade
& Laid
But O, Lord above,
have pity on my
missin kitty

## 22ND CHORUS

Usta smear ma lips with whiskey
  Fred and open up the doors
  to make a joke—while
   women waited
   and Bert Lahr waited
   playing what he waited
    like Duke Ellington

used to sit staring at Seymour
who implied to me the swing
   of the music by his
          low crash
          high abidin
                shoulders,
                P a p,
        and what wow hoo?

T h o t l a t n a p e
     Compose Vehicle
          Special
          Banana
           Nine

## 23RD CHORUS

Bat bow
lack Jack
swing Bing
that's right!
Yes
backwards—wail—
You're gut okay man
swing on along
I don't care
I can do it
  too
Orlak + +
    see

## 24TH CHORUS

If you once
 for all good
  times
Man's fine,
    know
YOU KNOW

## 25TH CHORUS

My mind! even harder than
    my path, my freedom
    is in piano
O, wow, wild wow
  NBC OOO
    piano
Like Lee Konitz
    sky,
Yay, wow?
    Sluke!
Slow! Swing? THEN
  YOU GO—
That new tenor cat
made me drop my pencil,
    Elvin Jones

## 26TH CHORUS

Zoot Sims
  and his
    Johnny Williams
"This Happy Leaping Thing"
Kitty Drum Barry
Gray, you like cemetary
    swing?
"Big Xmas Seal"
Hockey teams—?
Al? —shape
lay, & the Elington
Good high school
    sex orgy
      girls
    in the woods
      of
    rape,
    nun dear

## 27TH CHORUS

The New Orleans New York
Club
wishes to announce
the opening
of
new sessions,
& new fields, Daddio,

Dave Brubeck's
the swingingest

And I wish to say
Farewell
to
Al
Smith

Hello Dave

## 28TH CHORUS

For Minors Only
is the name of a new record
all about trumpet
& trimban

Zlap
Peter Orlovsky
is the cat to play to

You see dont you dig
on all sides
the wild sounds?
and o the conceptions
you made
on
Thursday
afternoon

trumpet man, dont blow
that thing at me,
blow it to
banana

## 29TH CHORUS

Timmy got back,
    soft Blakey lamb

Timmy got back
        & wrote rhymes

And we sat purring on the bed
    with Tammy

And made it 5 percent
    thousand

Times a day, swinging,
  we had sand,
  We had Gothic top
      Cathedral girls

  But O in Euniceburg
      they footballed
  Stupid me from Edgar
      Lear's interior
  Majesty

## 30TH CHORUS

No, this lamby bit
Is what I mean

O Orlando, O sweet

No Orlander phonecalls
    Georgia Flowerbranch

Lamby mean, William,
  Lamb dust? Nnaaa!
  Softy uglu flutey?
    Almost—

Pan flute Erdic
  Shook spear
  that Venusian cunt
   was neat when
    I'se a Nigger
      was
        a
        baby

## 31ST CHORUS

O Gary Snyder
we work in many ways

In Montreal I suffered tile
and rain

In Additional Christmas
waylayed babes

In old crow Hotels
full of blue babes
in pink dressinggowns
down

But O Gary Snyder,
where'd you go,
What I meant was
there you go

In Montreal I worked a manied-way

And, better than Old Post,
I learned t'appreciate
in many ways
Montreal, Soulsville,
and Drain

## 32ND CHORUS

Listening to a guy play
tenor saxophone &
keep the tune inside
chords & structures,
as sweetly as this,
you'll experience
the same
fitly thrill
you got from Mozart

It is pure musical beauty,
like a musicale
among wigs

People who dont understand
jazz are tone-deaf
& dont understand
what tone-deaf &
simply deaf
meant to Ludwig

## 33RD CHORUS

van
Beethoven

*

Goats as soft as break
of day
In swamp
Mexico

*

Can diamond cut iron?
Diamond cuts glass
glass links

But can it cut
An iron link?

Nirvana means Cut-Link

If diamond dont cut glass
or iron dont count,
hey?
maybe the Wisdom Vow
o the Diamondcutter
may have made it

## 34TH CHORUS

The only responsibility to a child
is to feed, the rest is
interference

Can you just see
a man arrested
for letting his daughter
fuck
around the block
anyway
anywhere
just so long as she got
home to eat her
dinner, he's telling
the cops
absolutely that

And the girl gets married?
I have a bunch of stray cats
in my yard

I wouldnt *have* a daughter

## 35TH CHORUS

Whattayouwanta have er for
You wanta sling sperm
over her?
Avin her now, ey you
old reprobate

Lissen, just keep that daughter
away from my knees
after she's thirteen

And between ten & that
tell her to lay off
the rough stuff

With boys you can play
as rough as you want,
but once ye spank em
they hate you forever

Oi Karamazov!

## 36TH CHORUS

O Apollo

Men

are the beautiful

The women miss cats

Cads & rogues
of Montreal all,

or blue diers in deep pars
asking for golfscore

But in any Case
tsa united press

## 37TH CHORUS

Old dotin old fuck

There's this old man,
he come down this road
just a walking with some
a whatyamaycallit
in a big bottle

& I dont know what was in it
& it come night
& I was in my house
& here come this old man
down the road
drinking outa that bottle
And there was Allen Wayne
in his house

## 38TH CHORUS

& he had to hang this sheet
on the clothesline

& that old man dropped
that bottle in his
yard

& that shu old man
dropped that bottle
down that road

And that's all,
Uncle Fred

## 39TH CHORUS

Maybe it's resting in the arms
of Jesus,
or just a cloudy windy day
In the trees

*

But since there's an infinite
amount of angels,
and Infinite ends in no 's,'
it must be
one angel

Infinites Angels?

Maybe that bird that floats
hill belly on the wind up there,
and that cat
that pats
in this grass,
is the same
Infinite
Worldwide
Angel

## 40TH CHORUS

A hard hearted old farmer
hidin his wine in the cellar

When he goes out he wears
earmuffs

He has a doublebitted axe
sharp enough
to shave shit

His people are all buried
in the same cemetery,
which is located
under the doorstep
where the boy
couldnt get through
from the tomb

## 41ST CHORUS

If we do battle,
Monsieur,
And you lose,
I gain nothing,
And if I lose,
you gain
Satisfaction

This is what the peasant said
when the aristocrat
challenged him to a duel

Women move slowly
but they dont stop

Europe, weep in your gloomy
rain

I brought it to him
so I could get you
in Paradise

## 42ND CHORUS

Abraham, drinking water by the tents

Pacing up & down the soft sand
under the stars

Worrying about Villages

Wondering if your vision was real
or just a foolish importunity
in your mind.
Yet moving on in the morning anyway
with the rattle of pack asses.

Abraham, the dew is in your beard
Abraham my eyes are open
You are weird

Abraham they've brought you
Your rooftops are mended

Your women bend no more
their heads under the sleepy
tentflap, & goats dont yew
& cry nomo in the singsong
tentvillage night

## 43RD CHORUS

Abraham I didnt write this right

## 44TH CHORUS

Dont ever come to Florida

A man was gettin up for work
& reached under his bed
in Kissimee
and a coral snake
bit him, February Florida
(lookin for his shoes)

A little boy playin in his yard
was et by a alligator
(true)

And an old lady dyin in her bed
was et up by fire ants
which found her
clean from the yard

And my mother saw a lizard
one foot long
on the garbage pail
that had big red eyes
(The fire ants went in
thru the mouth, man)

## 45TH CHORUS

There's a middlewestern prurience
about Greeks.—

Your little earth-nut, O potato
war, riots mama dears around
  papap's paternal root

S i l k y b o o

( o o ! )

Found the Sound

## 46TH CHORUS

Hollywood boy sing dog song
Dont be fooled by gun car
Or shine in hat of Sheriff
Cochise,
    or turn that dial,
    boy, you know whats happen
    to you when yard dog
    bit your fame

Yair, & dont sweep any leaves,
  Watch me play basketball
      I guess—

      In Inverness, where I'sa
        played hogball since
          your pappy skinned
                —Okay, old
                suit, see
                ya more

## 47TH CHORUS

Airplanes dropping barrels
  of shit on the White House
  On Roosevelt's very head
What do the women know
    of the wood?

All they gotta do is get drunk,
  Honorary Mayor

Up sprang the butcher boy
with the spring old man!

Why'st the fool play thou?

Because fools always follow.

  Followest what?

Because fooly are always follying?

    Nay, Sire, it was forgotten
  in that body's balconeer

## 48TH CHORUS

God ushered me into my house
What a batting champeen
honorable American Navy
Sweetheart God is to us
Japanese Rigour Girls

Buy that, Moke!

Dazz, I'ze innerested
in drape fall circus
and yo, yo got childrees
pleak okomiko bonny
sugar, ah, sweet,
dont let Robert Burns
burn that cigar of yours
Or mice lay men
to diamondshine
your kittlepee poopoo
Grace,
Otherwise purd
Hurt
New Year

## 49TH CHORUS

Way out
But not too way out

Barefaced wretch—
you're a pretty nice
barefaced wretch—
as bare faced wretches

go

T r u e  T o y !

Great day in the morning,

Ugh-y!

## 50TH CHORUS

Hollywood, if you want
little girls raped by sex
fiends, dont hint with
symbols, give it to me
  S t r a i g h t

Otto was pretty miserable
He chased little girls
  to rape in sawdust
  apartments yet unbuilt

He was a ugly big Otto
  but O when I was
    a little girl I loved
      all that

The lovely maniac
makes me smile

## 51ST CHORUS

Who is going to get rid
of his discriminating mind,
which is the way to
heaven, when he is being
eaten by crocodiles?

By means of his extremely
slow metabolism he was
enabled to keep far
on the father light,
far from the energy
particle of the mother

Ah, it's a depressing situation:
we imagine that
we live and imagine
that we die, too bad,
too bad

Manly manly manly friend
says the faggot on T V

## CERRADA MEDELLIN BLUES

(FIRST SOLO)

### 1ST CHORUS

Even when I was a little boy
I was always alone
with my guardian angel

Playing Tarzan
An icicle fell on me
& cut my arm
I had a rope around my neck
I was hanged in Innifree
Had my hand cut off in Perfidee
Never had my fill
of Thee

ST MICHAEL IN THE CORNER,
NINE FEET TALL

2ND CHORUS

The Only One
said Christ to me
When you're alone in Heaven
with God
Who is my Father
and Thine
You'll know that your self
you
And your guardian angel,
One,
And the self of any
Is
The Only One—
Sad Bent Head
in "Cant-Get-Away
From-That-Innisfree"

## 3RD CHORUS

I wonder what's hiding
in the Cross?
Did Jesus free the world?
Before him there were murders
officially.
From body to effigy
went history.
Emily Dickinson me that,
Thomas Hardy.
Roll me a pearl me
that, O Big Sur Sea.
And you, Ferlinghetti,
how do you like that
For rhyming free
Free of a doctor's degree.
Jean Louee.

## 4TH CHORUS

When I drink Bénédictine
I drink what the Holy
Father
Blessed
I drink the blood of Christ?
Naw!
I drink Christ hisself—
I say "Thank ye, God"
and drink—
And kiss the bottle
With the Cross on it
And D.O.M.
the director of drinkers—
The Heavenly Daiquiri?
The troublesome Innisfree.

## 5TH CHORUS

What's all this Innisfree
Running straight thru me?
Was Yeats invented it?
Or O'Shawn the Yurner?
Repetitive old rolling
smoke balloons?
Paul Newman's mouth
with Spanish ladies
arguing?
What?——Some truck?
Some cigaree? Halles
Market onions are free?
My Guardian Angel's
About to tell me—

## 6TH CHORUS

Alone with my Guardian Angel
  Alone in Innisfree
Alone in Mexico
                City
Alone with Benedict,
  Cave is free,
      alone is alone,
    Thou Only One—
  Alone and Alone
    The song of the pree
(Pree means prayer
 in English & Frenchie)
Choose yr words lightly,
      shit on the world,
   Merton'll die
      when he reads
            this from me

## 7TH CHORUS

I love Lax
A regular Pax
I love Lax
not Ex Lax
but
you see
Now Lax
But's teeth ne'er held
The comedian so grand
As them Lax horse teeth
Held prayer
to ground
Lax is a singer
Lax is a goner
Lax is a gonna
get mad onner

## 8TH CHORUS

My hand is moved
by holy angels
The life we are in
is invisible
Holy Ghost

If you could see me,
hoodlum,
You'd be Saint
Cant slash
at a loser
For Oy Yai O Paint
—Those lies are for liars
And me I'm a liar,
So liars forget
the handsome beget
The ugliest pricks
The angel beset

## 9TH CHORUS

But I stopped to think
The angel dont care
Nine feet tall
Beside the wall
Wants me cut out
To do the rub out
But I got fathers to care for
Father Shoyer is one
Father Gioscia is two
That's enough for you
—Ah Lucien
Al Jalisco
Ah I'm drunk
borracho

## 10TH CHORUS

Too drunk to write
Cant see the light

It's a strange thing when nuts
  get together
To form one cock—
  Young girls should shudder
    in that empty light—
  The holy of angels,
    I wonder what's he think?
  Shd push pencils
      for agers, masagers,
Masseurs and all?
  Oll? Lovely bedoodlers
    in Time's Holy All
Holiest Ghostliest
  ramified Hall

## 11TH CHORUS

And, said I to the Angel,
that *shall* certainly do,
And the Angel said:
D you remember Gregory?
Corso, the Way of Poetry?
Orlovsky too?
And Ginsberg O Shay?
And Burroughs the Master
speaks thru his teeth?
And the writer of story
the generous Honkey?
And Lafcadio the Holy
Innocent of Russia,
the Patriarch, & Sebastian?
And Lucien?
And Neal Cassady?

## 12TH CHORUS

Move my hand Lord
move my hand
Tell Ray Bremser
something calm him
down
Tell Leroi Jones
& Diane di Prima
tooo
They dont know
that Heaven
which is waiting for them
In the land of OO

(SECOND SOLO)

## 1ST CHORUS

"You can think by yourself"
  says God from Heaven
Talking to all 70 thousand
  Billion Four Thousand
  Eighty Two Trillions
  of Creatures in his Movie
called "Creation"

(pause)

2ND CHORUS

He means that all
those sentient beings
are free to think unimpeded
—Only God is the Only One
who knows that all the thinking
going on
is what the thinking going on

is thinking

And none of it ever happened

SHTMIMK!

Shtmimk?

## 3RD CHORUS

But like any other movie
the thinking is gray
but also big romances
like Latin Love You music
& all of it seems so golden
steada gray.
That's because it's a very strange
movie
It is strange as dulcet gray.

Hey looka me Ma
I'm writing like Yorkshire
Pudding De-Headed Gray
The proof is in the pudding
they Bray
Just like any other old Canaday

## 4TH CHORUS

The brain is a pudding
with raisins in't
Hey looka me Ma I'm thinking
like Otay—
Okay, Mémo,
Está bien, Mémo,
Parandero.

(That's what they mean Espanish
'Hey kiddy, dont hit
the bars too much,
chico.'

Hey Baby dont yup at me
in Azmetec!)

Yair, Pard old Hoopard
Hoomingway blew his head

over Old I-day-o

## 5TH CHORUS

Hemingway Blues, is called.
Me too Blues—You Blues
—Thinkin Blues—Paris
Blues and Blacks—
Hurshy, move the tack!
Dont bring me no le-mon
chiffin, pie, man,
I'll break yore head in

Head already broken in
No chin
Yes chin
Soft Chin
Northport Autumn
falling leaves blues
And winter white
sailboat philosopher
blues, on sand,
Lois and Victor by name.

## 6TH CHORUS

All kindsa fine blues
even this minute
in Vera Cruz,
Terre Haute,
Montana,
Golgotha,
Heaven Door.

All kindsa information rattlin
back & forth
Crazy old angel midnight
world talkin singin
rubbin antennaes
High on antenni
and go Mondadori'n
in Italy for to see sweep
of Gary Venice Door's
Venetian oar

## 7TH CHORUS

Or go Atyastapafi'n
in other planets?
Goo, what a gaw!
And does wet boulders think?

I see the face of Christ
in the door
after it has been the face
of the Dog, the Owl,
the Lamb, the Lion,
Christ, the Dog again,
the Collie then suddenly
my God the Colleen!
Her soft brown eyes,
esperanza morena,
Then it's Christ again,
this time in profile
—This I just saw.

## 8TH CHORUS

I'm now going into a deep trance
where I see visions—
Mwee hee hee ha ha.
Johnny Holmes is just about
the funniest man I know!
He laughs in cemeteries
in the woods of Connecticutt

(Connect ton cul, we used
to call
it
in little
Canada.)

Connect your arse.
Some come on John, connect
your arse to a Grave,
pal, almost lover, and
I'll bring ye sweet
daydrids
in the morning
of the 2 thieves & Me

& You

## 9TH CHORUS

(Written before I knew about Pascal —1965)

But John's like Pascal,
or like Frank O'hara even,
He wont let his head
Believe his heart
& all that
So he skeptically adjusts
his glasses, leans forward eagerly,
almost hugely,
& roars

Qui à poignez
ton cul dans
terre!

And 2 days later he looks it up
in a French Dictionary,
wondering what I'm thinking
about, and what I think
about him thinking.
Wow Very Strange

## 10TH CHORUS

It's dillier than that
they daisies they pud
in puddinhead blues.

To Earl of Shockshire:
"Sire, in this my Inscribe
May't you'll fee."
The Earl of Shrockshire
shires & showers & shh's
on back a batch
of Tanguipore
Tangled
Telegrams
Mistaken by Saint Peter
as Hair of the Gate

# NOTES ON DATES AND SOURCES

"San Francisco Blues"
In a letter to Allen Ginsberg, Kerouac referred to writing this poem in March 1954, when he "left Neal's . . . and went to live in the Cameo Hotel on Third Street Frisco Skid Row."

"Richmond Hill Blues"
Written in Richmond Hill, New York, while Kerouac was living with his mother. He began the poem on September 4, 1953, and completed it later that month.

"Bowery Blues"
Kerouac dated the poem March 29, 1955.

"MacDougal Street Blues"
Kerouac dated the poem June 26, 1955.

"Desolation Blues"
"Desolation Peak
Mt. Baker Nat'l Forest
Washington State
August 1956"

"Orizaba 210 Blues"
"Written in a tejado rooftop dobe cell
at Orizaba 210, Mexico City, Fall 1956
. . . by candlelight . . . "

"Orlanda Blues"
Begun in July 1957, finished February 17, 1958, this poem was written in Orlando, Florida—"Orlanda" in native parlance.

"Cerrada Medellin Blues"
"July 1961
37–A Cerrada Medellin
Mexico, D.F., Mexico"
Begun in June, finished in July.

*Book of Blues* is one of the unpublished manuscripts Jack Kerouac left in his meticulously organized archive. It does not contain all of Kerouac's unpublished blues poems—he chose not to include, for instance, "Berkeley Blues," "Brooklyn Bridge Blues," "Tangier Blues," "Washington DC Blues," and "Earthquake Blues." Comparisons with Kerouac's original handwritten notebooks indicate that in the process of editing the book he deleted and rearranged some verses, and made some small editorial changes. Readers familiar with the excerpts from "San Francisco Blues" published in *Scattered Poems* and the excerpts from "MacDougal Street Blues" published in *Heaven and Other Poems* will notice that Kerouac subsequently made changes in some of those verses. Kerouac's original typescript of *Book of Blues* is located in the Henry W. and Albert A. Berg Collection of English and American Literature, the New York Public Library, Astor, Lenox and Tilden Foundations.

I have taken the liberty of dedicating this book on Jack's behalf to two of his close friends and correspondents, Philip Whalen and Lew Welch.

—John Sampas,
Literary Executor, Estate of Jack and Stella Kerouac

## JACK WOULD SPEAK THROUGH THE IMPERFECT MEDIUM OF ALICE

So I'm an alcoholic Catholic mother-lover
yet there is no sweetish nectar no fuzzed-peach
thing no song sing but in the word
to which I'm starlessly unreachably faithful
you, pedant & you, politically righteous & you, alive
you think you can peal my sober word apart from my drunken
  word
my Buddhist word apart from my white sugar Thérèse word my
word to comrade from my word to my mother
but all my words are one word my lives one
my last to first wound round in finally fiberless crystalline skein

I began as a drunkard & ended as a child
I began as an ordinary cruel lover & ended as a boy who
                read radiant newsprint
I began physically embarrassing—"bloated"—&
                ended as a perfect black-haired laddy
I began unnaturally subservient to my mother &
                ended in the crib of her goldenness
I began in a fatal hemorrhage & ended in a
                tiny love's body perfect smallest one

But I began in a word & I ended in a word &
                I know that word better
Than any knows me or knows that word,
                probably, but I only asked to know it—
That word is the word when I say me bloated
                & when I say me manly it's
The word that word I write perfectly lovingly
                one & one after the other one

But you—you can only take it when it's that one & not
some other one
Or you say "he lost it" as if I (I so nothinged) could ever
lose the word
But when there's only one word—when
you know them, the words—
The words are all only one word the perfect
word—
My body my alcohol my pain my death are only
the perfect word as I

Tell it to you, poor sweet categorizers
Listen
Every me I was & wrote
were only & all (gently)
That one perfect word

—Alice Notley